G000056650

WORKING SPACES
TODAY

LINKS

WORKING SPACES TODAY

Edition 2014

Author: Carles Broto

Editorial coordination: Jacobo Krauel

Graphic design & production: Roberto Bottura & Oriol Vallès

Cover design: Oriol Vallès, graphic designer

Text: Contributed by the architects, edited by Naomi Ferguson

© LinksBooks

Jonqueres, 10, 1-5

08003 Barcelona, Spain

Tel.: +34-93-301-21-99

info@linksbooks.net

www.linksbooks.net

© This is a collective work. In accordance with Intellectual Property Law "collective works" are NOT necessarily those produced by more than one author. They have been created by the initiative and coordination of one person who edits and distributes them under his/her name. A collective work constitutes a collection of contributions from different authors whose personal contributions form part of a creation, without it being possible to separately attribute rights over the work as a whole.

© All rights reserved. No part of this book may be used or reproduced in any manner whatsoever without written permission except in the case of brief quotations embodied in critical articles and reviews.

WORKING SPACES
TODAY

LINKS

INDEX

007 Introduction

008 Clive Wilkinson Architects
JWT Headquarters, New York

018 group8
Cargo

024 Sprikk
Ynno Workplace

032 Patrick Tighe Architecture
Moving Picture Company Headquarters

042 Shubin + Donaldson Architects
WongDoody Offices

050 Elding Oscarson
NoPicnic

060 NAU + DGJ
Raiffeisenbank Zürich

066 i29 l interior architects
Gummo Offices

074 Iwamoto Scott
Obscura Digital Offices

086 za bor architects
Yandex Kiev Offices

094 za bor architects
Forward Media Group Publishing House Offices

100 Gensler
United Business Media

108 FLATarchitects
Nije Gritenije

118 Nendo
Meguro Offices

126 Taranta Creations
Red Town Offices

132 facet studio
Studio Spec

138 Essentia Designs
Dentsu London

146 Studio SKLIM
Thin Office

156 Bottega + Ehrhardt Architekten
Publicmotor Brand Communication

164 Jackie B
Cubion a/s Offices

174 Abeijón-Fernández
MAXAN

182 COEN!
Kapero Offices

190 GPAC
Saegeling Medizintechnik

200 Coen
Besturenraad / BKO Offices

208 Bates Smart Architects
Media House

216 Elding Oscarson
Oktavilla

222 SUE Architekten
Prayer Rahs

228 Cannon Design
The Power House Renovation/Restoration

236 Kling Stubbins
Autodesk AEC Headquarters

242 Skylab Architecture
NORTH Office Interior

248 nhdro
The Black Box

256 Randy Brown
DATA

262 Origins
Onesize Offices

270 Albert France-Lanord Architects
Pionen – White Mountain

276 Crea International
CheBanca! Branch Offices

284 Ippolito Fleitz Group
Agencia Bruce B./Emmy B.

294 Johnson Chou
Red Bull Canadian Headquarters

The work environment, as a space for professional and interpersonal exchange, has undergone dramatic changes in recent years. The continuing swift pace of developments in communication technology, with a new, more timeless, ubiquitous and portable handling of information, has greatly contributed to these changes. Gone are the bulky filing cabinets and expansive tables of yesteryear, with work surfaces having been reduced to the size of a computer. Tele-work and video-conferencing are further indications of this omnipresence.

At the same time, however, there is an ever-increasing trend towards sustainability in architecture, as evidenced by energy-saving measures, alternative energy sources and the use of new materials.

These, and a host of additional concerns particular to office design, greet the architect and interior designer when drawing up the plans for a new workspace. The company's corporate identity, for example, must be somehow translated into the design of the interior spaces, as well as infusing the building as a whole. The modern office also requires versatility and dynamism – it must be flexible enough to quickly adapt to a range of uses. It must be aesthetically pleasing and should encourage interpersonal communication among employees, whilst significantly lessening outdated hierarchical barriers.

This volume, which brings together a wide range of examples of renovated spaces as well as new build projects, comprises an invaluable source of inspiration and an in-depth study of the challenges involved in creating new workspaces.

Clive Wilkinson Architects

JWT Headquarters, New York

New York City, New York, USA

Photographs: Eric Laignel Photography

JWT, formerly J. Walter Thompson, is one of the oldest and largest advertising agencies in the world. While its credentials and client list were impeccable, the company needed to transform itself to meet the challenges of the new media world. Youthful new leadership at the New York headquarters determined to make that a complete physical, virtual and behavioral transformation. In June 2004, Clive Wilkinson Architects was appointed to design the transformation with workplace strategists, DEGW, assisting with client visioning, and HOK New York providing executive architect services. With a total workforce of 900 people, JWT occupied 250,000 sqft (23,200 sqm) in 5 floors of the office building at 466 Lexington Ave. The floors were sequentially gutted, remodeled and reoccupied in four construction phases over three years, with final completion occurring in February 2008.

From inception, it was clear that JWT was reframing its core vision about how it engaged with the public. Advertising would no longer focus on projecting messages to the consumer, but creating experiences which rewarded the public's time and attention. Its mission had become 'story telling'. To promote interaction, mobility and collaboration, the isolated divisions within JWT would be opened up and reconnected. The new space would be 'open architecture', with no private offices, and vertical movement between floors would be facilitated to unite the JWT community. Separate businesses, such as the post-production facility JWTwo, would be expressed as distinct but integrated companies, adding character to the space.

The architectural concept became a thematic thread: the design team used the tree as a metaphor for storytelling and extended it as organizing form and connective tissue between the individual branches of the agency. This 'narrative tree' links all floors: the 'trunk' is the atrium void and staircase that connects all floors over the main entrance hall. The 'branches' are ovoid shaped meeting rooms: either solid green cones, or acoustically padded green tents. The cones are angled, like branches stretching through floors.

This architectural expression is most dramatic on the lowest floor, level 2, which benefits from 18 ft high ceilings. The entry atrium here stretches to 32 ft high with a concrete staircase winding through it. As circulation off the stairs flow into distinctive 'neighborhoods' representing various departments within the agency, special landmarks such as meeting and conference rooms help create visual interest while facilitating way-finding. The creative area includes a mezzanine 'tree house' structure with several collaboration spaces and an adjacent multi-purpose café/bar space with an illuminated bar. The mezzanine is painted NY taxi yellow to match the taxis visible though the window on the adjacent Grand Central overpass. Since undertaking the transformation, JWT has seen a slew of business wins and associated expansion.

Architecture:
Clive Wilkinson Architects

Project team:
Clive Wilkinson,
John Meachem,
Neil Muntzel,
Hailey Soren, Lindsay Green, Daniella Oberherr,
Nicole Sylianteng, Yana Khudyakova,
Jacqueline Law

Executive architect:
HOK NY

Client:
JWT NY, formerly J. Walter Thompson NY

Floor area:
250,000 sqft (23,226 sqm)

FLOOR PLANS:

1. Conference room
2. Small meeting room
3. Lounge
4. Open workstations
5. Office
6. Elevator lobby
7. Reception area
8. Town hall / café
9. Bar
10. Restrooms
11. Pantry
12. Copy / print
13. Servies / systems
14. Mail
15. Storage
16. A/V production
17. IT

+3 floor plan

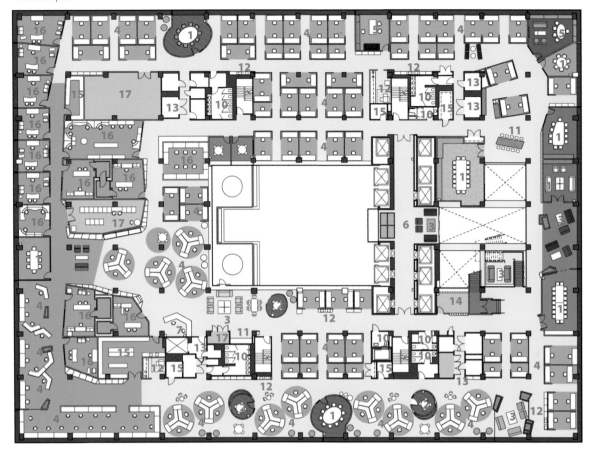

+2 floor plan

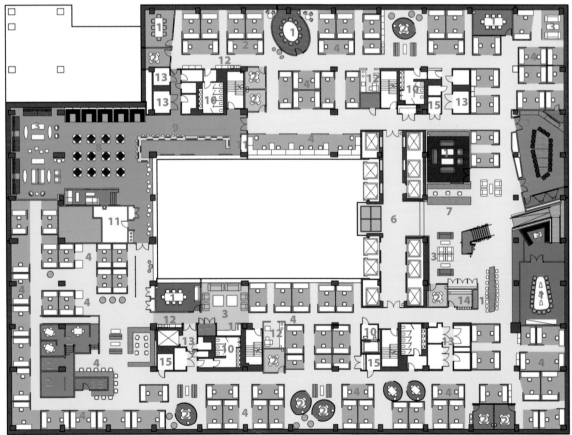

13

FLOOR PLANS:

1. Conference room
2. Small meeting room
3. Lounge
4. Open workstations
5. Office
6. Elevator lobby
7. Reception area
8. Town hall / café
9. Bar
10. Restrooms
11. Pantry
12. Copy / print
13. Servies / systems
14. Mail
15. Storage
16. A/V production
17. IT

+5 floor plan

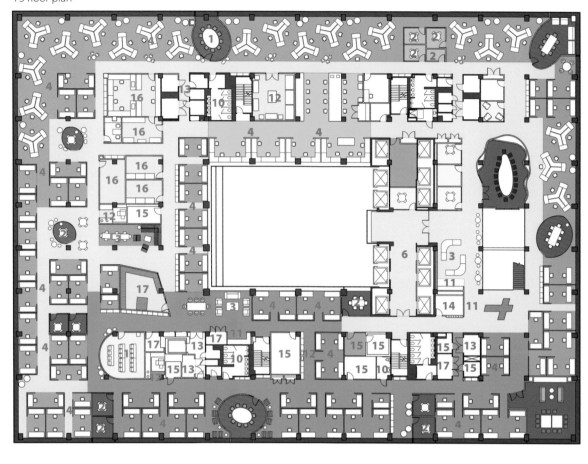

+4 floor plan

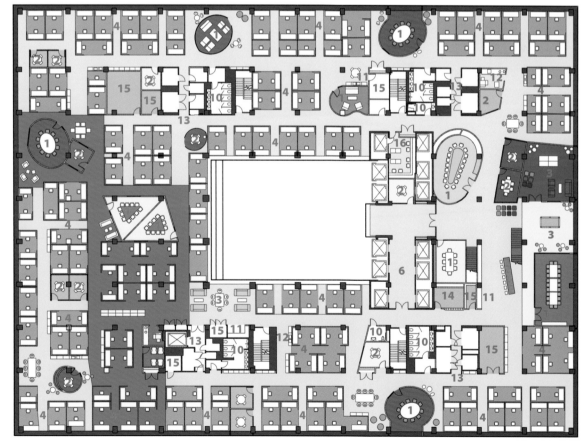

The new space is open plan, with no private offices, and vertical movement between floors has been facilitated to unite the JWT community.

group8

Cargo

Geneva, Switzerland

Photographs: Régis Golay, Federal Studio

With branches in Europe and Asia, the architecture firm group8 celebrated its 10th anniversary by opening a new office location in Geneva, Switzerland, known as the Cargo. The aim of the design was for the new offices to embody the studio's spirit and identity.

The offices are housed within a former industrial warehouse, close to the center of the city, and have been designed to take full advantage of the building's 8,395 sqft (780 sqm) of floor space and 30 ft (9 m) high ceilings.

The white and luminous warehouse space contains a hidden treasure: 16 recycled shipping containers, all of which have traveled thousands of miles around the globe. These silent travelers are piled up like giant Lego bricks, left, in fact, as they were found, without any changes made to their exteriors. The aesthetic maintains the poetry of their former use and differentiates them from the immateriality of the large neutral space they lie in.

On a practical level, the use of containers represents a gain of 2,150 sqft (200 sqm), and makes excellent use of the ceiling height. Following the concept of artist Marcel Duchamp's "readymades", these monumental objects have acquired a new function. Modern objects and industrial space both recover a functional use which turns them into contemporary living and working spaces. The containers formalize structured collective spaces. Each container embodies a collective form or a work-related situation: meeting rooms, cafeteria, lounge zone, bathrooms and showers, etc.

The other half of the scheme is in opposition with the containers' structured zone: an open space enlightened by natural light that pours in through the glass-roof. This informal meeting space gathers all the employees together, thereby generating a strong sense of synergy in the workplace. This second zone is composed of informal meeting spaces (exchange spaces) that are radically differentiated from the containers' intimate interiors.

The white open space gives shape to a neutral environment, which aims to encourage creative work. The white furniture lends a spatial rhythm through its differentiated skyline, like a small city inside the city. The non-repetition of patterns in the furniture design gives birth to a kind of miniature landscape, far away from the habitual rigid office environments.

Architecture:
group8

Project team:
Christophe Pidoux, Christian Giussoni, Richard Fulop, Marco Neri and Diana Alvarez

Total surface area:
8,395 sqft (780 sqm)

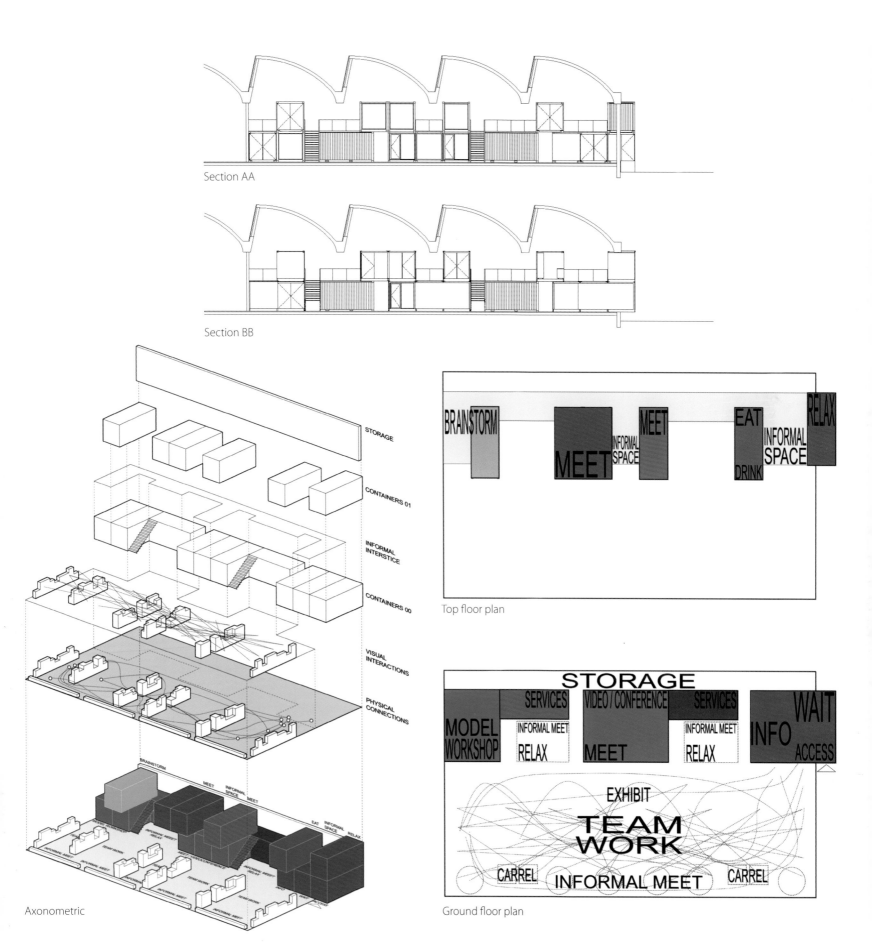

Section AA

Section BB

STORAGE

CONTAINERS 01

INFORMAL
INTERSTICE

CONTAINERS 00

VISUAL
INTERACTIONS

PHYSICAL
CONNECTIONS

Axonometric

BRAINSTORM MEET MEET EAT RELAX
INFORMAL SPACE DRINK INFORMAL SPACE

Top floor plan

STORAGE
SERVICES VIDEO / CONFERENCE SERVICES WAIT
MODEL WORKSHOP INFORMAL MEET MEET INFORMAL MEET INFO
RELAX RELAX ACCESS

EXHIBIT
TEAM WORK
CARREL INFORMAL MEET CARREL

Ground floor plan

The idea of using readymades has to do with recycling objects without transforming their aspect. It is also a reference to the industrial past of the building.

Sprikk

Ynno Workplace

Utrecht, the Netherlands

Photographs: Edward Clydesdale Thomson

Sprikk designed a new working environment for consulting agency YNNO. YNNO advises on innovative methods of working and the environments that support these. Their expertise follows the conceptions of "new ways of working". Sprikk planned their office to embody these notions.

Since their consultants spend more time at their client's place of work than in their own office, YNNO asked for a workplace that functions as a home base rather than a conventional office. A working environment was created that suits the nature of the consultant's way of working in which communication and networking play a vital role.

The floor plan is kept entirely open with the exception of two acoustically separated glass volumes. This stimulates free movement, spontaneous encounters and flexible uses while allowing for lots of natural light.

In this open plan, organically shaped birchwood structures were placed that form partitions, niches, storage spaces and bookshelves. By applying one material and a single construction method, a coherent appearance of the space is created that still offers a diversity of working places with gradations between open and closed environments. The natural, haptic qualities of these birchwood structures form a contrast to the high-end communication and presentation technologies that were applied throughout the space.

The wood structures contain a number of ergonomic workplaces that embrace daylight and offer a view to the outside. Settings for the concentrated individual as well as active collaboration can be found. A vis-à-vis setting for casual discussions is placed on a platform integrated into the wooden structures. Groups of up to eight people can work on projects and presentations in an acoustically well-balanced room. The room is fitted with writable surfaces and high-end presentation equipment. Private meetings or presentations for clients are held in an acoustically separated room that offers a casual atmosphere and plenty of daylight.

Architecture:
Sprikk

Design team:
Johan van Sprundel, Max Rink, Klaas Kresse

Contractor:
Steenland Interieurbouw B.V.

Client:
YNNO B.V.

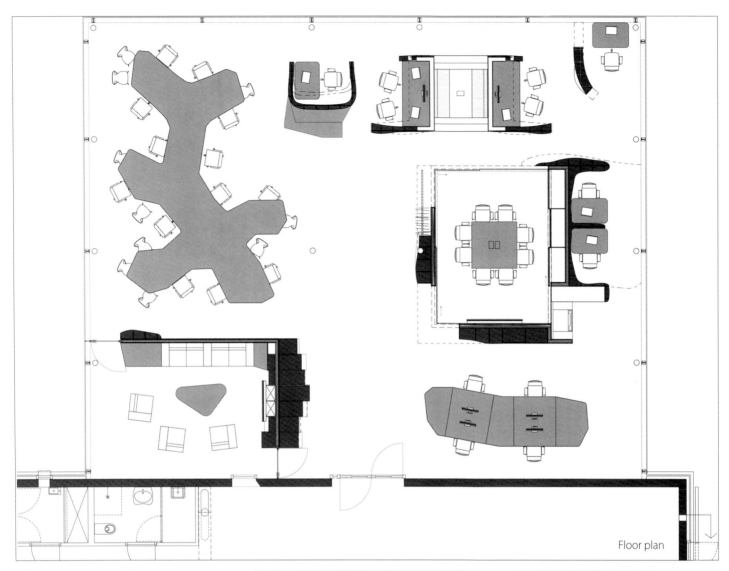

Floor plan

A free-formed wooden island, close to the printer and the archive, can be used for secretarial and administrative work but can also function as an open office desk space for the consultants.

Sprikk created a workplace that suits the client's wish for a unique and exciting work environment that contributes to YNNO's identity as a young and innovative company.

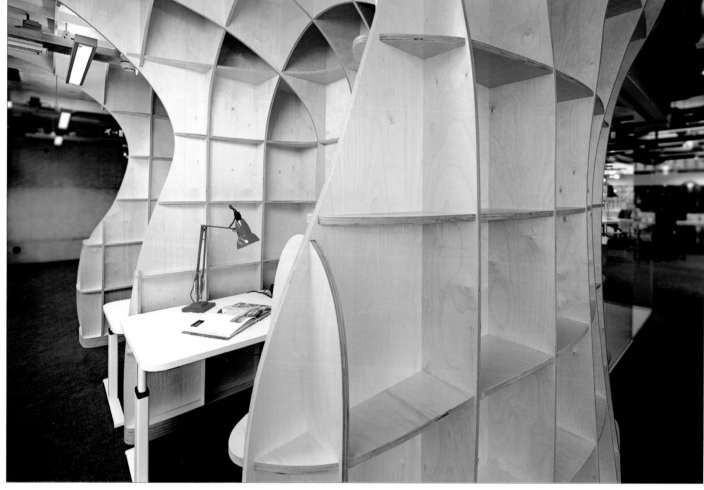

Longitudinal section

Patrick Tighe Architecture

Moving Picture Company Headquarters

Santa Monica, California, USA

Photographs: Art Gray Photography

The 7,800 square feet (725 sqm) visual effects post-production facility is located within a generic office building in downtown Santa Monica, California. The Moving Picture Company is a UK-based visual effects post production company, a forerunner in the visual effects and animation fields for the feature film, advertising, music and television industries. The facility serves as the United States headquarters. The company is highly regarded for its work in the field of color manipulation in film. With this in mind, the project explores the notion of light as it relates to color. The forms and patterns employed in the design have been generated through analyses and three-dimensional modelling of light patterns. Frames from the resultant animation sequence have been selected and layered to organize spatial qualities and movement through the office environment.

An organic, sinuous spine weaves its way through the suite. An appendaged soffit grows from the serpentine walls and serves as an armature for cable trays, mechanical and electrical systems. Light portals equipped with programmable LED lighting pierce the organic forms. Patterns derived from the animated studies are emblazoned onto the laser cut walls and circumscribe the interior.

Movement is expressed throughout the space in many ways, one of which is through the lighting scheme. Clusters of LED lights penetrate the serpentine wall and emit color. The custom-made aluminum housings are flush with the outer (public) face of the wall and protrude into the private rooms, adding texture to the walls and creating a more intimate scale within the larger spaces. The intensity and colors of the lighting are programmable enabling the client to fulfill one of the items on their 'wish-list': the creation of an environment in constant flux.

Grading rooms, Editing bays, Conference rooms, open and closed offices, client areas, production spaces, entertaining areas, the tape vault, mechanical rooms, machine rooms, exterior terraces and support spaces make up the program of the facility.

Architecture:
Patrick Tighe Architecture

Floor area:
725 sqm (7,800 sqft)

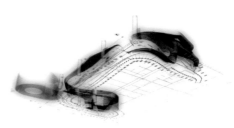

The Moving Picture Company is highly regarded for its work in the field of color manipulation in film. With this in mind, the project explores the notion of light as it relates to color. The forms and patterns employed in the design have been generated through analyses and three-dimensional modelling of light patterns. Frames from the resultant animation sequence have been selected and layered to organize spatial qualities and movement through the office environment.

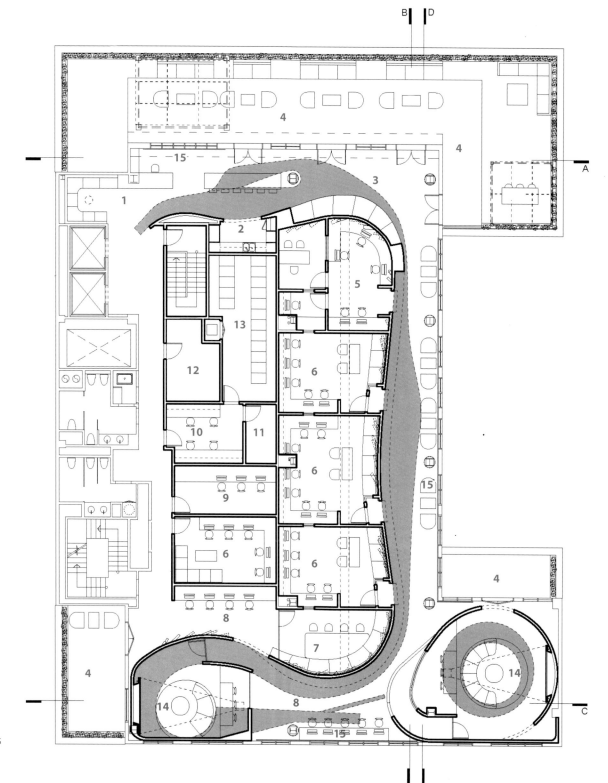

FLOOR PLAN

1. Lobby
2. Kitchen
3. Common area
4. Terrace
5. Office
6. Project room
7. Conference room
8. Open office
9. Edit room
10. Tape op roo
11. Scan
12. Film / tape
13. Machine room
14. Grading room
15. Aluminum laser-cut panels

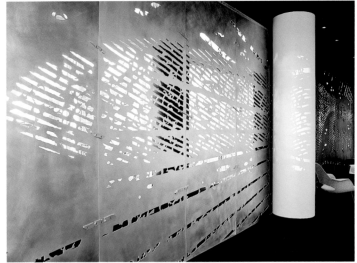

Frame sections

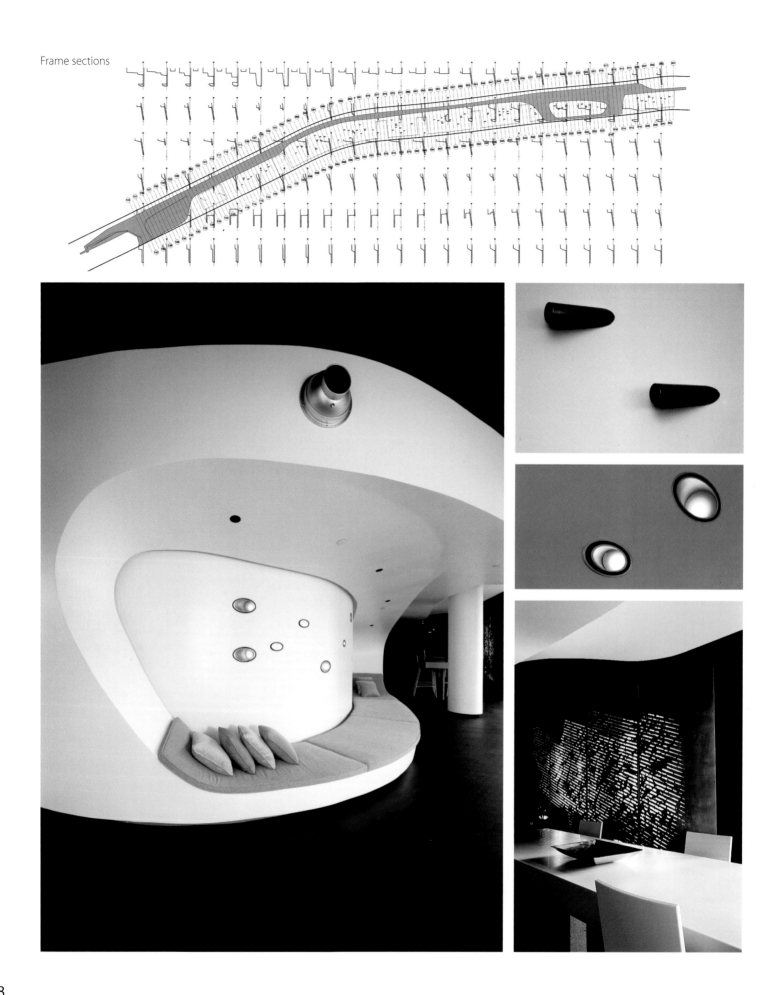

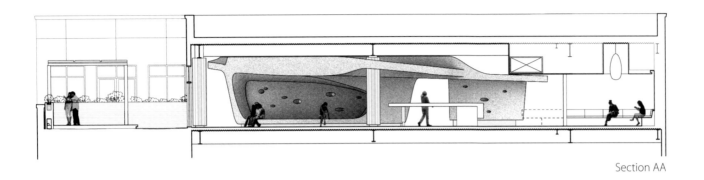

Section AA

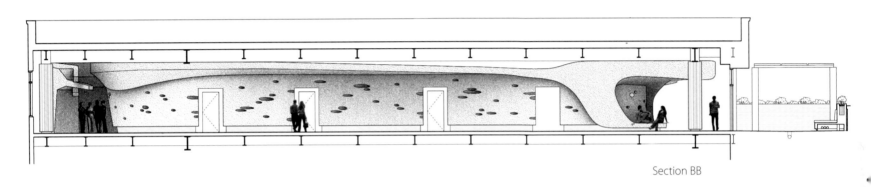

Section BB

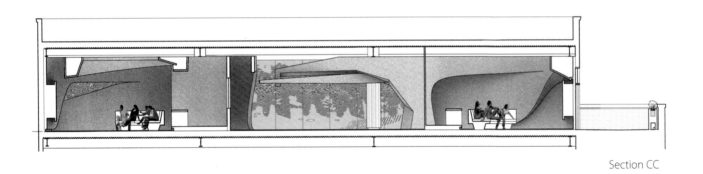

Section CC

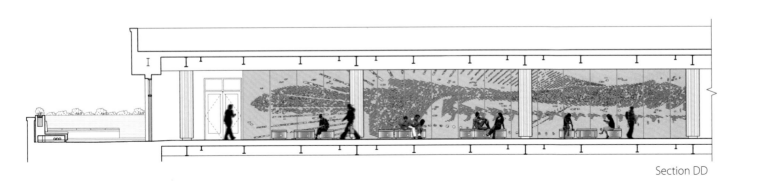

Section DD

Shubin + Donaldson Architects

WongDoody Offices

Culver City, California, USA

Photographs: Tom Bonner

WongDoody wanted an office space that would communicate the agency's ideals to prospective employees and clients. The company wanted the interior architecture to tell the story of WongDoody's values and reason for being. There were several Key concepts for the design: a democracy of ideas, fun, continuous improvement, the development and cultivation of relationships with clients and colleagues, and that the space reflect the quality of work that WongDoody produces.

The Los Angeles office of WongDoody is the adaptive reuse of a former warehouse. While the shell of the building was mainly left unchanged, the interior construction partitioned the space to accommodate the company's needs. The space is organized into three wings: a public wing flanked by two private work wings. All four of the public meeting/war rooms—the cork room, green room, black room, and silver room—are in the center of the space, marked by rectangular enclosures of different materials. The private work wings include the creative zone, interactive zone, communications, administrative, and account executives areas.

The building used to be a beer shipping facility with immense refrigerated compartments. The architects retained the large, zinc refrigerator doors, incorporating them into the new design. These original doors were used at various locales, including the main entrance into the facility and at the conference room, where the doors can be opened to bring in natural light that penetrates the room's slotted roll-up aluminum door.

All of the workstations remain open to the soaring, bow-string truss wood ceiling, while a perimeter of original brick surrounds the space. A combination of skylights and vertical recessed fluorescent lighting illuminate the facility. The original concrete flooring remains throughout all of the circulation and production zones of the space. Cork flooring accentuates the reception, kitchen, and lounge areas. Very directional, linear-patterned carpeting covers the remainder of the work areas.

The walls of the war rooms are dual functioning. In addition to enclosing the meeting spaces, they are clad in varying materials that can be used to develop ideas. Cork exteriors can be used for pin-up purposes; silver dry erase clad exteriors are ready for ink; chalkboard-painted walls of green and black are set for jotting notes or sketching ideas.

Architecture:
Shubin + Donaldson Architects

General contractor:
Speer Construction

Structural engineer:
John Labib and Associates

Mechanical engineer:
Air Products

Electrical engineer:
California Industrial

Lighting designer:
Lighting Design Alliance

Gross area:
13,800 sqft (1,280 sqm)

Total staff size:
60

Total cost:
$1.2 million (Construction: $925,000;
Furniture: $270,000)

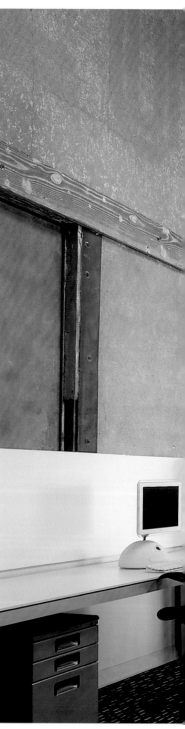

There were several key concepts for the design: a democracy of ideas, fun, continuous improvement, the development and cultivation of relationships with clients and colleagues, and that the space reflect the quality of work that WongDoody produces.

Floor plan

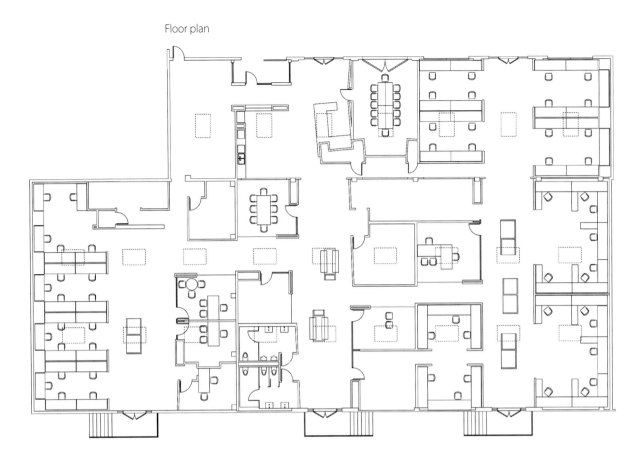

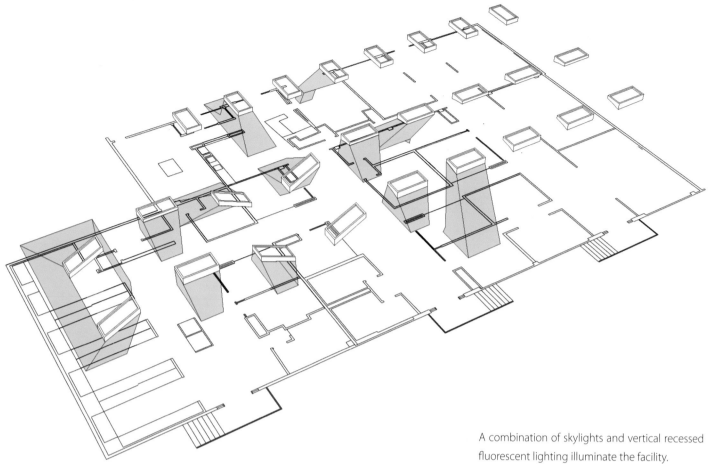

A combination of skylights and vertical recessed fluorescent lighting illuminate the facility.

Elding Oscarson

No Picnic

Stockholm, Sweden

Photographs: Åke E:son Lindman

Architecture:
Elding Oscarson
Gross area:
1100 sqm (11,840 sqft)

No Picnic is one of the world's largest design consultants, covering industrial design, product design, and packaging design as well as art direction, consumer insight, and architecture. The architects could hardly imagine a better informed client, and expected nothing less than an ambitious, demanding, and fun project. The client wanted large, open office spaces, a prototype workshop, a prototype showroom, several project rooms and a customer area, separated from the other spaces in order to maintain privacy. The client had found a group of 19th century buildings in central Stockholm of which the two principal volumes – a former exercise hall for troops and a stable for police horses – were listed in the historical buildings register with the highest degree of protection. They had been converted into showrooms in the 1980s and were in a sad state of repair. Their conversion had to be realized with extreme sensitivity, so much so that the architects have evaluated every step with a historic buildings specialist, literally down to each new screw hole.

The buildings have been stripped of all additional layers down to the original building fabric. In the old stable block they were able to strip the room, and added only a custom designed acoustic treatment along the walls, but in the exercise hall, economy and function demanded that a mezzanine constructed in the 1980s was kept. The mezzanine cut the hall lengthwise, destroying the experience of the space. Its edge coincided with the center of the hall, so the architects opted for a method used in industrial design – recreating the illusion of the hall as a whole space by reflecting the half that had been preserved intact, by constructing a delicate aluminum wall along the hall's central axis.

The meeting rooms behind the metal membrane have large windows overlooking the hall. The flat reflection of the glass flush with the distorting metal surface makes the glass seem like a mirror while the metal appears transparent: the wall is there, yet it disappears. It is bold, kaleidoscopic and illusory with its trompe l'oeil effects. At the same time it allows the main act to take center stage: the light and space of the exercise hall and the old building's straightforward display of materials, construction, imperfections, and the passage of time.

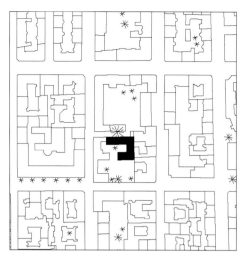

The design consultants, No Picnic, commissioned Elding Oscarson to convert a group of 19th century buildings in central Stockholm into their new headquarters with large, open office spaces, a prototype workshop, a prototype showroom, several project rooms and a customer area.

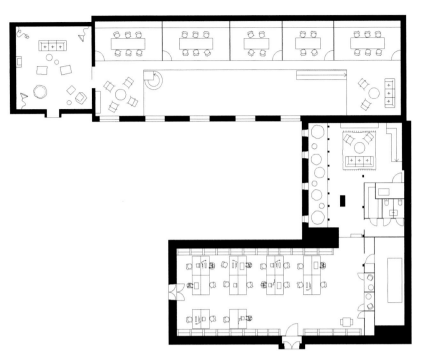

First floor plan

The former exercise hall for troops and stable for police horses were listed in the historical buildings register with the highest degree of protection so the conversion had to be realized with extreme sensitivity, so much so that the architects have evaluated every step with a historic buildings specialist.

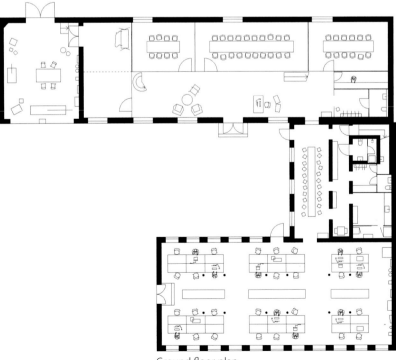

Ground floor plan

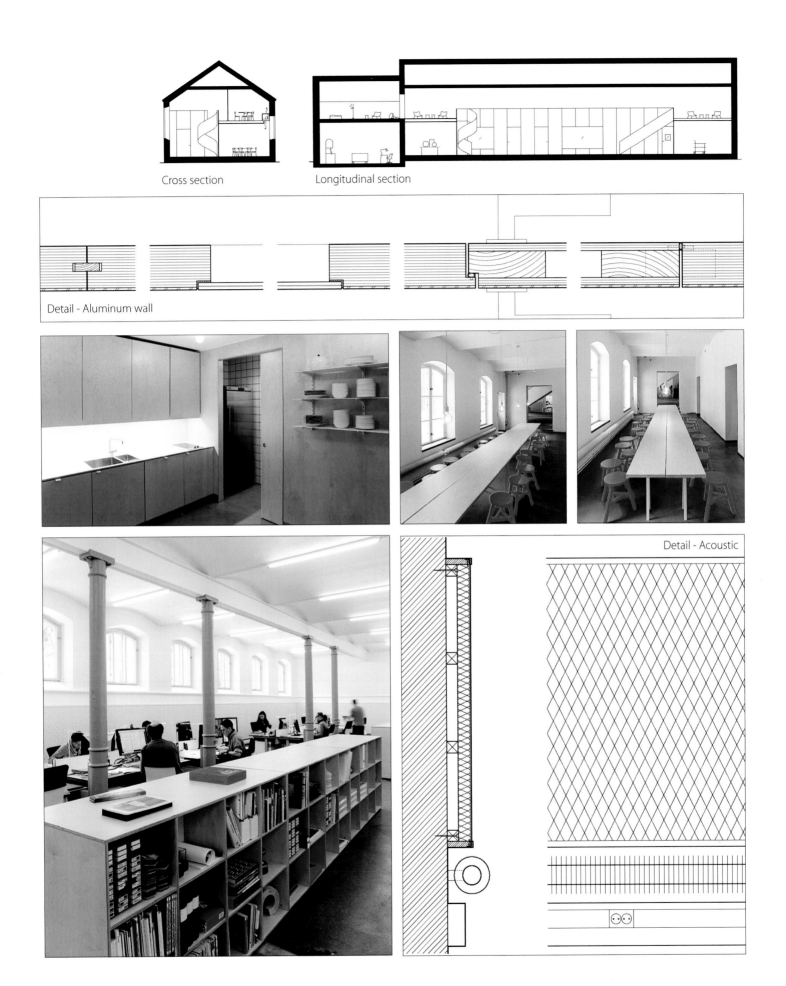

Cross section

Longitudinal section

Detail - Aluminum wall

Detail - Acoustic

NAU + DGJ

Raiffeisenbank Zürich

Zürich, Switzerland

Photographs: Jan Bitter

Raiffeisen's flagship branch on Zurich's Kreuzplatz dissolves traditional barriers between customer and employee, creating a new type of "open bank," a space of encounter. Advanced technologies make banking infrastructure largely invisible; employees access terminals concealed in furniture elements, while a robotic retrieval system grants 24-hour access to safety deposit boxes. This shifts the bank's role into becoming a light-filled, inviting environment – an open lounge where customers can learn about new products and services. This lounge feels more like a high-end retail environment than a traditional bank interior. Conversations can start spontaneously around a touchscreen-equipped information table and transition to meeting rooms for more private discussions. The information table not only displays figures from world markets in real time, but can be used to discover the history of Hottingen or check the latest sports scores.

Elegantly flowing walls blend the different areas of the bank into one smooth continuum, spanning from the customer reception at the front, to employee workstations oriented to the courtyard. The plan carefully controls views to create different grades of privacy and to maximize daylight throughout. The walls themselves act as a membrane mediating between the open public spaces and intimately scaled conference rooms. Portraits of the quarter's most prominent past residents like Böklin, Semper or Sypri grace the walls, their abstracted images milled into Hi-macs using advanced digital production techniques. While intricately decorative, the design grounds the bank in the area's cultural past, while looking clearly towards the future.

Architecture:
NAU
DREXLER GUINAND JAUSLIN ARCHITEKTEN
Construction supervision:
Archobau
Quantity surveryor:
PBK
Digital fabrication:
Rippmann Oesterle Knauss
Mechanical engineer:
PGMM Schweiz
Electrical engineer:
Mosimann & Partner
Lighting design:
Sommerlatte & Sommerlatte
Construction engineer:
Henauer Gugler
Acoustics:
Braune Roth
Media:
iart interactive

Raiffeisen's flagship branch on Zurich's Kreuzplatz dissolves traditional barriers between customer and employee, creating a new type of "open bank," a space of encounter. Advanced technologies make banking infrastructure largely invisible; employees access terminals concealed in furniture elements, while a robotic retrieval system grants 24-hour access to safety deposit boxes. This shifts the bank's role into becoming a light-filled, inviting environment – an open lounge where customers can learn about new products and services.

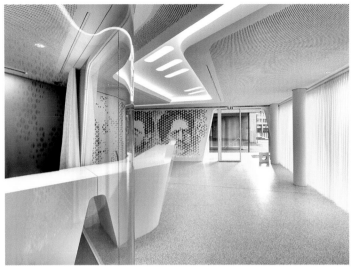

FLOOR PLAN

1. Entrance/ATM
2. Safety deposit access
3. Lobby/reception
4. Cash desk
5. Lounge/info-table
6. Meeting room
7. Offices
8. Director's office
9. Break room
10. Secure zone

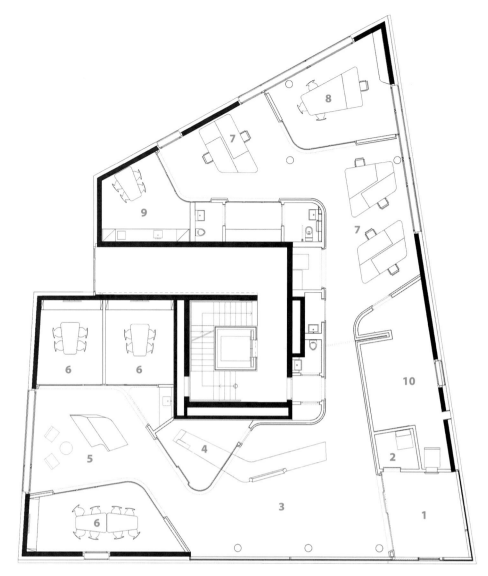

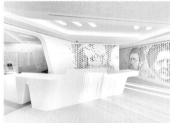

i29 l interior architects

Gummo Offices

Amsterdam, the Netherlands

Photographs: i29 l interior architects

Gummo is an independent full-service advertising agency based in Amsterdam. i29 l interior architects are a creative and versatile design studio whose aim is to create intelligent designs and striking images. As the space on the first floor of the old Parool newspaper building in Amsterdam was only going to be rented by Gummo for two years, i29 convinced Gummo to embrace the mantra of "reduce, reuse, recycle" to create a stylish office space that would have as small an impact as possible on the environment or on the client's wallet. The architects developed a theme that would reflect Gummo's personality and design philosophy – simple, uncomplicated, no-nonsense, yet unquestionably stylish with a twist of humour. Everything in the office conforms to the new house style of white and grey. All the furniture was locally sourced via Marktplaats (the Dutch eBay), charity shops and whatever was salvageable from the old office. Everything was then spray-painted with Polyurea Hotspray (an environmentally friendly paint) to conform to the new colour scheme. Even Jesus wasn't immune, as you can see in the attached pictures. The new office is a perfect case study of a smart way to fill a temporary space stylishly and at minimal cost. The new coating has given the collection of old and repaired items an exciting new potential. i29 l interior architects have created a new area in fashionable corporate responsibility for the Gummo advertising agency.

Architecture:
i29 l interior architects

Walls/ceiling:
concrete / panelled ceiling

Custom made furniture:
synthetic coated mdf

Furniture:
synthetic coated second hand furniture

Constructor:
Stefan Klopper

Coating:
Krimpex Coating systems (hotspray)

Surface area:
450 sqm (4840 sqft)

Floor plan

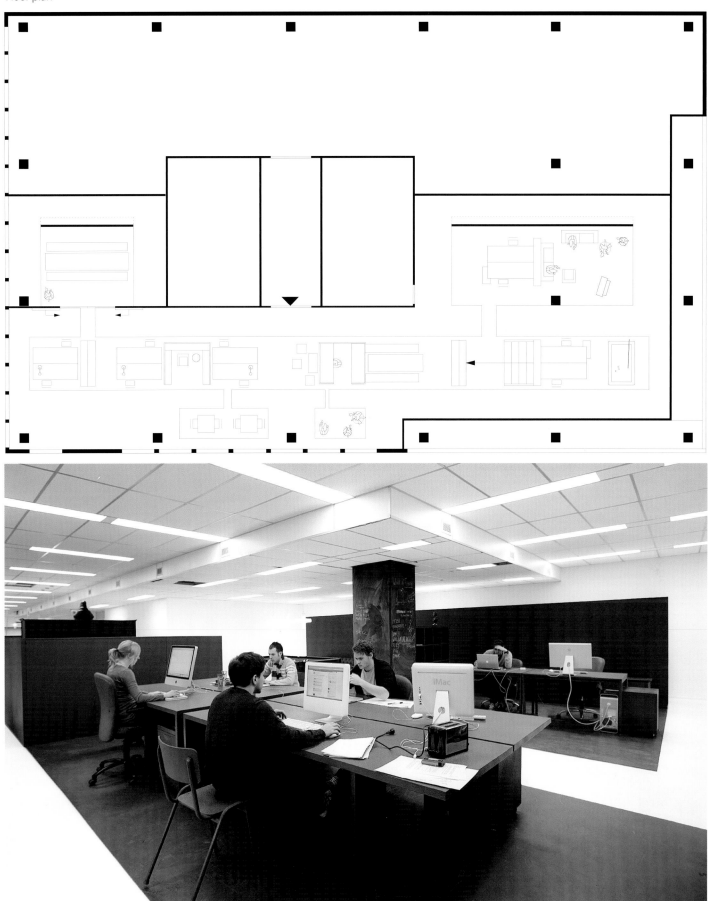

PROCESS

1. A wide open space.
2. The office layout is determined by the floor patterning. First white, then gray.
3. The Kringloopwinkel, a second-hand furniture shop in West Amsterdam. Great furniture for a great price.
4. Coloring in...
5. On Marktplaats, the Dutch eBay, we found a piano for 20 euros.
6. The office was furnished with items from Krigloopwinkel, Marktplaats and Ikea.
7. The Quissam family were moving, so put their set of Chesterfield sofas up for sale. The designers picked it up the day after Ramadam, Eid so made the most of the opportunity to taste every Morrocan delicacy going.
8. Three lorries were sent to Krimpex in Krimpen a/d ljssel with everthing they'd acquired for the office.
9. Krimpex sprayed everything with an indestructible solvent-free RAL 7024 (Grey to you and me) color coating.
10. When they were done, the three lorries, now full of gray furniture, returned to Amsterdam.
11. The ultimate test - Tommaso finds out if the Krimpex can withstand a fiery Italian temperament and boiling water.

All the furniture was locally sourced via Marktplaats (the Dutch eBay), charity shops and whatever was salvageable from the old office. Everything was then spray-painted with Polyurea Hotspray (an environmentally friendly paint) to conform to the new color scheme.

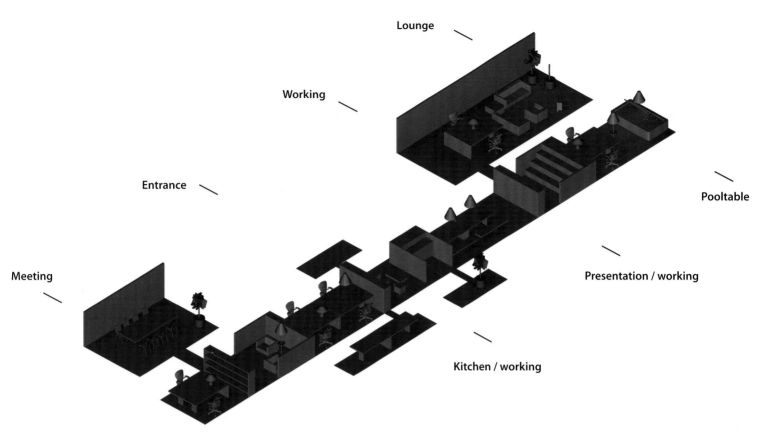

Lounge

Working

Entrance

Pooltable

Meeting

Presentation / working

Kitchen / working

IwamotoScott Architecture

Obscura Digital Headquarters

San Francisco, California, USA **Photographs:** Rien van Rijthoven & Iwamoto Scott Architecture

Obscura Digital, a ten year old well-recognized immersive and interactive media company, recently relocated from their former headquarters to these 36,000 sqft premises with interiors designed by IwamotoScott. The project called for innovative construction techniques and materials to meet the very strict budget and schedule constraints while still offering a unique design that reflected the company's cutting-edge artistic ethos.

Obscura's work involves design, r&d, fabrication and installation across a range of digital media, including architectural projections and large interactive touchscreens. Programmatic requirements for the space included an office and meeting space for the partners and staff, a large multi-functional showroom and exhibition area, workstations for digital production, and prototyping workshop spaces. The new space is within a three-story 1940s concrete and steel framed warehouse in the Dogpatch neighborhood of San Francisco. The prototyping workshop and showroom are located on the lower level, the reception, main offices and meeting spaces on the middle level, and production on the top level. An important aspect of the redesign was the removal of three bays from the center of the building to form a spatial connection between the lower and mid levels. This move also allowed the installation of one of Obscura's hemispherical projection theaters housed within a 30 ft diameter geodesic dome. Overlooking this new double height space is a conference room designed as a freestanding object peering over the end of the new void, oriented towards the dome. One side of this 'meeting box' is kinked inward to adapt to the seismic bracing of the existing structure and create room for a stair that connects the two levels at the edge of the void.

A broad new staircase at the entrance allows an easy spatial flow into the reception area, partners' offices and central meeting space. Partner and staff offices are defined by twisting polycarbonate screen walls that allow filtered views as well as the transmission of natural light from perimeter windows and skylights above.

IwamotoScott Architecture shares the space with Obscura Digital, and their 1,100 sqft office is located at the eastern end of the main floor, behind the main building façade on Third Street. A digitally-fabricated book shelf and screen wall defines the edge of Obscura Digital's space, while providing a modulated projection surface facing the central space on which they can test out projection mapping techniques. The wall is made of an array of folded laser-cut steel modules following an oblique pixilated pattern that responds to the spherical geometry of Obscura's adjacent geodesic projection dome.

Architecture:
IwamotoScott Architecture
Floor area:
3,340 sqm (36,000 sqft)

© Rien van Rijthoven ▶

© Rien van Rijthoven

Programmatic requirements for the space included an office and meeting space for the partners and staff, a large multi-functional showroom and exhibition area, workstations for digital production, and prototyping workshop spaces.

© Iwamoto Scott Architecture

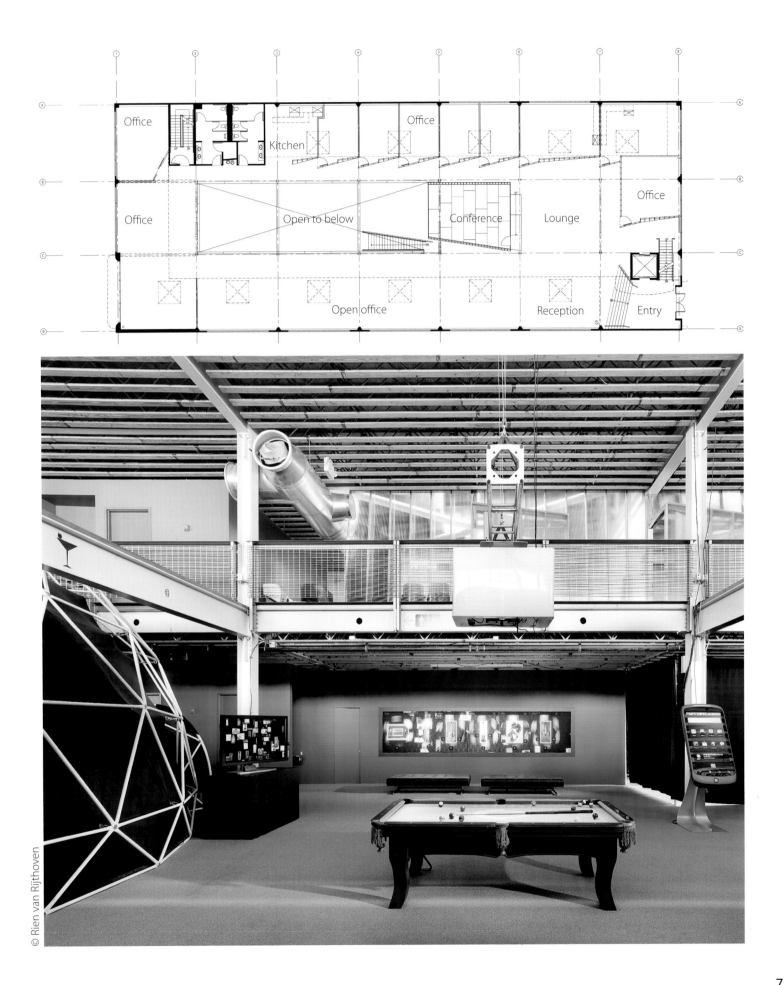

© Rien van Rijthoven

77

© Rien van Rijthoven

© Iwamoto Scott Architecture ►◄

© Iwamoto Scott Architecture ►◄

© Rien van Rijthoven ►◄

Overlooking this new double height space is a conference room designed as a freestanding object peering over the end of the new void, oriented towards the dome.

© Rien van Rijthoven

© Iwamoto Scott Architecture

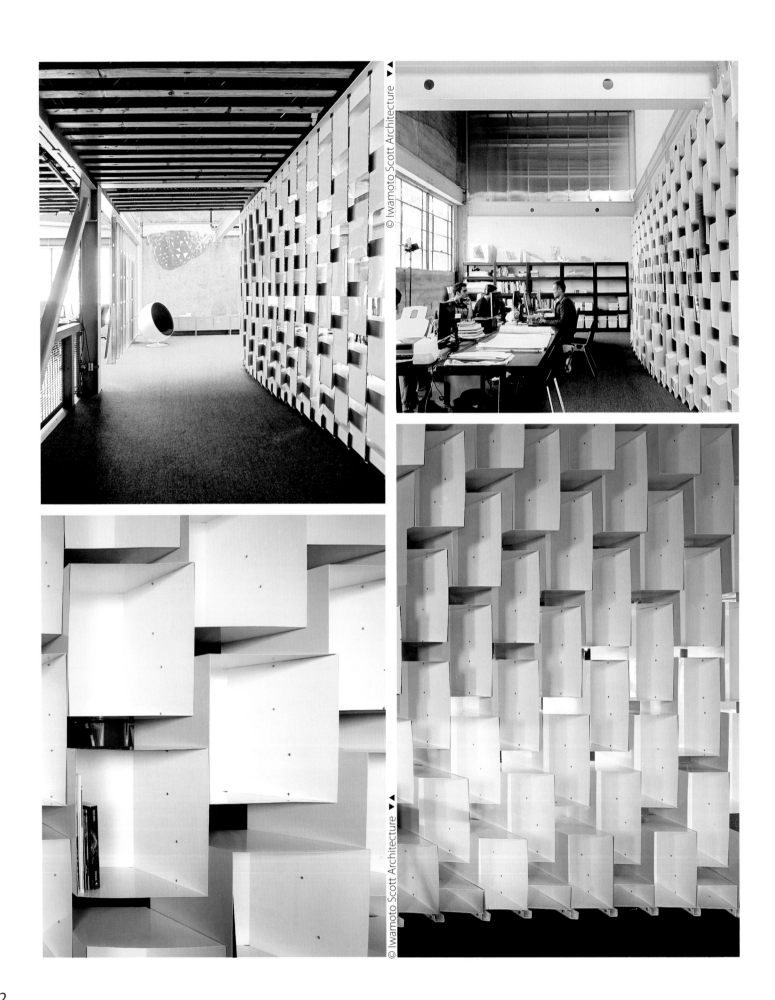

© Iwamoto Scott Architecture ▼

© Iwamoto Scott Architecture ▼

© Iwamoto Scott Architecture

© Iwamoto Scott Architecture

© Rien van Rijthoven

© Rien van Rijthoven

© Rien van Rijthoven

© Iwamoto Scott Architecture

© Iwamoto Scott Architecture

za bor architects

Yandex Kiev Offices

Kiev, Ukraine

Photographs: Peter Zaytsev

Architecture:
za bor architects

Project team:
Peter Zaytsev and Arseniy Borisenko

Project area:
290 sqm (3120 sqft)

Yandex, the company for which this office has been designed, is the most popular Russian internet segment search engine and one the world's top 25 sites. The company is constantly developing and in late July 2011 the Kiev branch of Yandex moved to new office premises. As with a dozen other Yandex offices it has been designed by the Moscow practice, za bor architects.

The architects, Arseniy Borisenko and Peter Zaytsev, commented on their priorities in the design: "We strive to make every project the most ecofriendly. It appears in the use of natural materials and the creation of user-friendly spaces: comfortable, quirky, cheerful ones; spaces which don't resemble dull gray offices in their standard plastic version. While developing the concept of the Yandex Kiev office we wanted to create a modern and welcoming space — that is, to infuse it with the qualities of the IT company, which is famous for the care it takes of its staff".

The offices were to be only 290 sqm in area, (the smallest office designed by the bureau to date), but the location of the project was very interesting. The offices occupy the sixth and seventh floors of the top-class Leonardo Business Center, a two-level space with a void. The space is well lit with natural daylight through a huge arched window which offers a wonderful view of the Kiev Opera House and the square in front of it. This unusual window informed the architects' decision to use large XAL lamps. While the offices, in contrast to other Yandex offices, do not contain a gym nor other recreational zone except for an oversized coffee-point, the internal distribution is very fluid and the space is not overloaded with workstations. Visitors are met at the reception area where they can wait for a meeting in contemporary Fritz Hansen armchairs. The reception area is finished in the corporate colors with the company logo. On each of the two levels there are about fifteen workstations equipped with ergonomic Herman Miller furniture. There are also two meeting rooms, the lower one used principally for meeting with clients while the upper meeting room is used for internal meetings.

The upper, mezzanine level, is fully glazed and connects to the lower floor via a staircase. The gallery and staircase were designed as a single sculptural form with particularly complex geometry. The design was explained to the contractors using a scale model, which was transported from Moscow to Kiev in deep winter during the construction works. The builders in Kiev successfully reproduced the exact geometry of the design. After completion, the builders reported that this was the most difficult job that they had realized to date.

6TH FLOOR

1. Reception
2. Conference room
3. Main work space
4. WC
5. Coffee-point
6. Support office
7. Closet
8. Communications

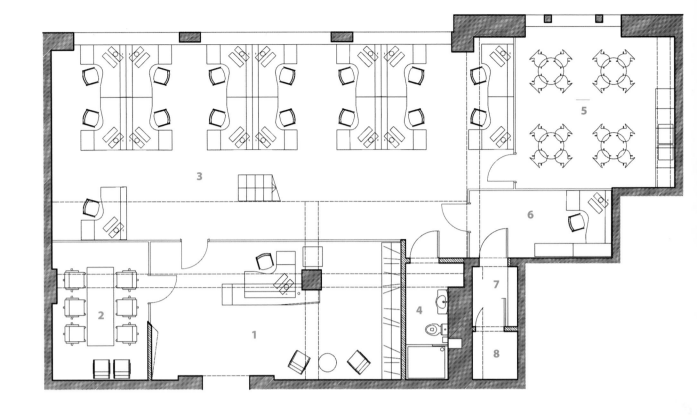

7TH FLOOR

 9. Hall
10. Conference room
11. WC
12. Sales department
13. Sales department

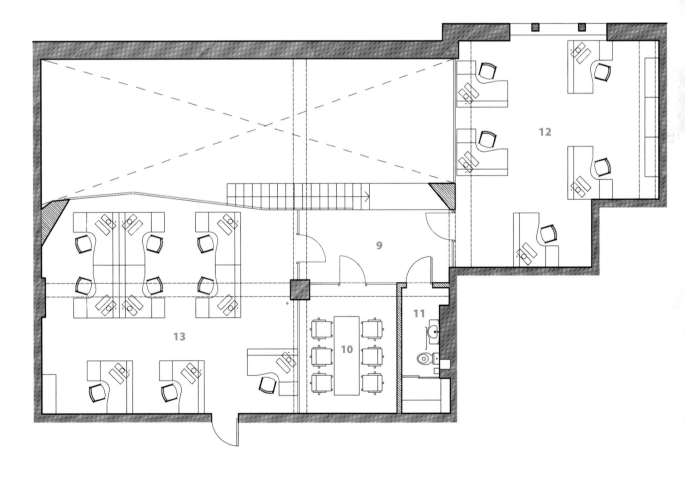

The gallery and staircase were designed as a single sculptural form with particularly complex geometry. The design was explained to the contractors using a scale model, which was transported from Moscow to Kiev in deep winter during the construction works.

93

za bor architects

Forward Media Group Publishing House Offices

Moscow, Russia

Photographs: Peter Zaytsev

In addition to several popular and well-recognized magazines such as 'Hello', Forward Media Group, owned by the Russian billionaire Oleg Deripaska, publishes the largest and the most popular magazines on interior design in Russia and Russian-speaking countries, including titles such as 'Interior+design', '100% Office', '100% Bathrooms' and '100% Kitchens'. za bor architects was chosen from among several thousand practices to design Forward Media Group Publishing House's head office in Moscow.

The project was clearly going to be fairly complex from the outset – the premises comprised a huge loft of 4200 sqm with a narrow, elongated plan, located in the mansard level of a new business center. The situation was further complicated by the particularities of the program – the need for open plan editorial offices as well as commercial and retail departments, separate offices for directors and editors-in-chief with a conference corner, conference rooms, an archive with a library, storage rooms etc. All of these facilities were placed along the corridor which runs the length of the space. Open plan workstations have been concentrated on one side, and cabinets located on the other side of the corridor. Key communal areas were designed to be transparent and distinctively identifiable. As a result, the elevator lobby, the bright reception areas and the meeting rooms were intentional points of emphasis in the design scheme. A yellow construction hides the entrances to the toilets while the archive room is decorated with a striking black floral pattern. In contrast, operational areas are finished in a neutral gray palette.

Architecture:
za bor architects

Project team:
Arseniy Borisenko and Peter Zaytsev

Project area:
4200 sqm (45,200 sqft)

A yellow construction hides the entrances to the toilets while the archive room is decorated with a striking black floral pattern. In contrast, operational areas are finished in a neutral gray palette.

■ Corridor

■ Service rooms

■ Work spaces

■ Editors-in-chief and heads of department office

■ Conference rooms

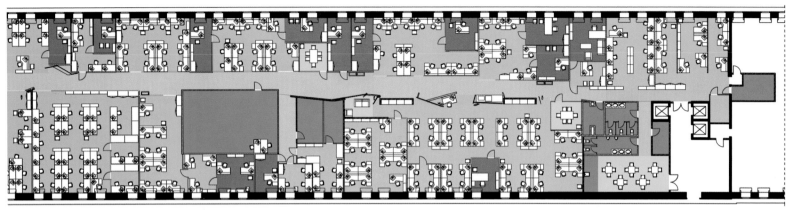

Key communal areas were designed to be transparent and distinctively identifiable. As a result, the elevator lobby, the bright reception areas and the meeting rooms were intentional points of emphasis in the design scheme.

Gensler

United Business Media

San Francisco, California, USA

Photographs: Nic Lehoux

Interior architecture:
Gensler

This global, 170 year old UK-based business media company shifted from print to digital early on in the internet revolution by embracing new technology. They had offices in San Francisco that represented the old, print based UBM: a warren of 8 x 10 ft cubes with high dividing panels. They wanted their new office to represent the innovative media company that they've become, while embracing the next generation of workplace thinking.

The space is located in a 1970s Brutalist office building that was designed for office and light industrial uses in the SOMA (South of Market) area of San Francisco, which has since become a focal point of "dot-com" companies. The angular floor plate presented challenges in plan. The designers decided to use the odd geometry to UBM's benefit – workstations are placed in the more regular, rectilinear areas of the plan, while meeting rooms and collaborative spaces take advantage of the plan's triangular oddities. The designers met the challenge of achieving a 75 sqft (7 sqm) per person metric by providing a completely open office environment that is complemented by gathering, amenity and meeting spaces. To relieve the density, there are two large communal spaces: the Town Hall and the Junction. They are strategically located to encourage gathering: the Town Hall opens onto a large outdoor deck and the Junction is placed at the knuckle of the floor plate. The Town Hall incorporates a café and elevated platform with a conversation pit that has jokingly been named the "dry hot tub". The platform leads out to a large deck that is surrounded by the views of the Bay and the downtown San Francisco skyline. It is a great place to relax or get fresh air on a nice day. The Junction features a second coffee bar with casual meeting places and spaces for relaxing.

Circular semi private "chat boxes", the name inspired by London's classic telephone boxes, are scattered through the open plan, giving the staff a cocoon for quick casual meetings.

The primary architectural element of the space is an angular, folding ribbon that moves through the space from floor to wall to ceiling and back to floor. The ribbon represents the quick flow and rapid interchange of information in the new media age. The flowing ribbon contrasts with the rigor of the workstations, ceiling system and lighting, which work with the building's structural grid. UBM wanted to reflect their global nature, while at the same time being respectful and inclusive of the local culture. Three San Francisco street artists and one installation artist were commissioned to work directly on the walls of the folding ribbon.

The lighting, building systems, equipment, appliances, furniture, materials and finishes all support the targeted LEED Platinum rating that is essential to UBM's mission of measurably improving their carbon footprint year to year.

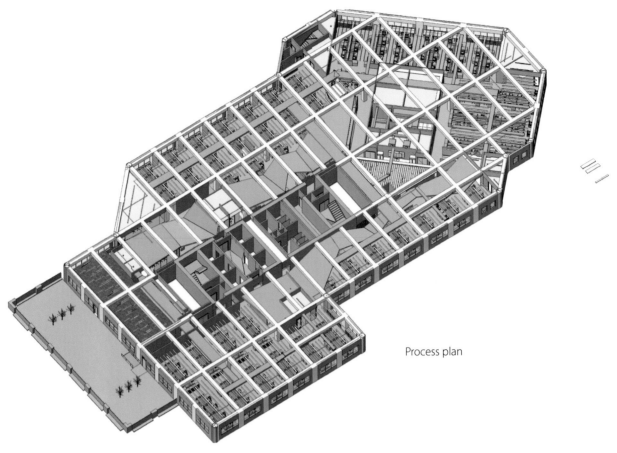

Process plan

103

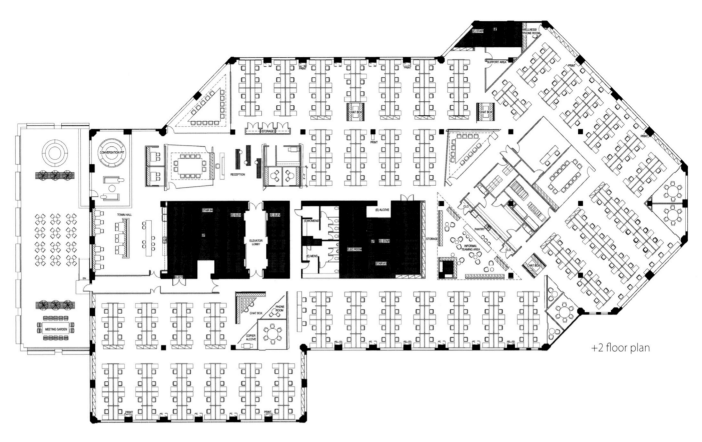

+2 floor plan

The "Town Hall" communal area incorporates a café and elevated platform with a conversation pit that has jokingly been named the "dry hot tub". The platform leads out to a large deck that is surrounded by the downtown San Francisco skyline. It is a great place to relax or get fresh air on a nice day.

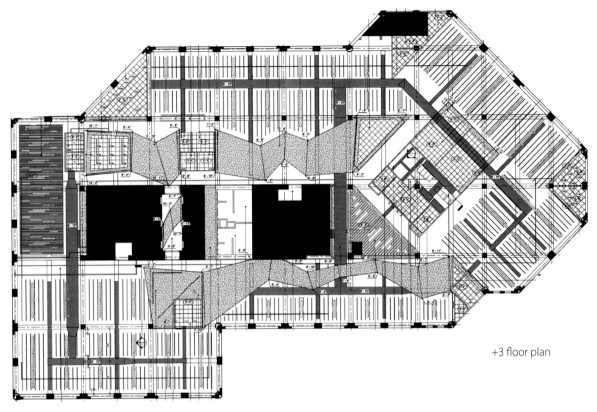

+3 floor plan

107

FLATarchitects

Nije Gritenije

Heerenveen, the Netherlands

Photographs: Arend Loerts

The Nije Gritenije foundation is a Rabobank initiative to stimulate local and regional entrepreneurship. The foundation asked Amsterdam based FLATarchitects to design twenty workstations and a conference room on the ninth and tenth floors of the brand new Rabobank building. Four of the workstations were to be used by the permanent staff of the foundation while the remaining sixteen were to accomodate a continuously changing group of start-up entrepreneurs and artists.

FLATarchitects devised a simple interior design which could be customized and completed by the users so that they could adapt their space to their specific needs. In this way temporary users are able to appropriate their place of work in a relatively short period of time. Also, the interior is designed to encourage innovation and discussion among users and visitors.

The stairs to the ninth floor end in an entrance space configured by four irregularly shaped objects. Together they form a 'porous wall', filtering views of and sounds from the workspace beyond. Through the gaps and reflective surfaces of the wall, sounds and images are presented to the visitor in fragments. The shifting sightlines of the visitor climbing the stairs were used as a design instrument for these wooden objects. These same objects are used as bookshelves on the side of the workspace.

The permanent workstations are positioned next to the entrance, in a fan layout with a shared drawer unit in the center. Their shapes and colors differentiate them from the flexible workstations. Four large tables provide space for the sixteen temporary workstations. The tables consist of a steel frame with a tabletop of steel grid panels. The tabletops can be arranged according to each user's needs by combining various desk elements, such as desktops of several sizes, storage objects, book displays and multiple sockets.

From the entrance space the stairs lead on to the conference and presentation room on the tenth floor. The carpeting dominates the space, covering parts of the wall as well as the floor. It displays a giant map of Friesland (the Dutch province) designed by graphic artist Martin Draax. The members of the Nije Gritenije foundation gather over this map, around a grand conference table with eleven chairs, one for each Frisian city. By drawing a curtain, part of the space can be dimmed for showing films or presentations. When looking out of the windows the real map of Friesland unfolds.

Architecture:
FLATarchitects

Leading designer:
Jos Blom

Client:
Rabobank Heerenveen-Gorredijk

Built area:
370 sqm (3,980 sqft)

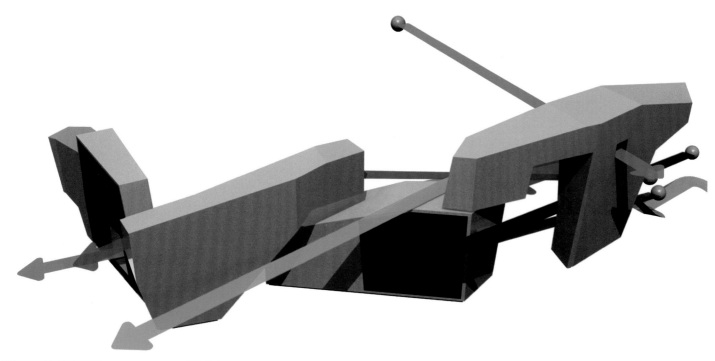

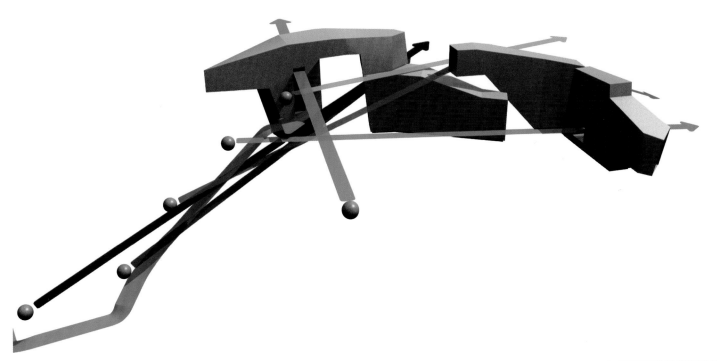

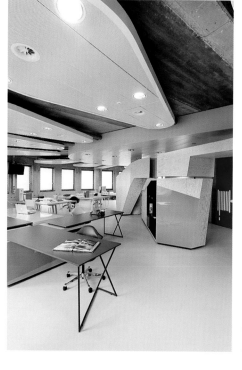

The entrance space is configured by four irregularly shaped objects. Together they form a 'porous wall', filtering views of and sounds from the workspace beyond. Through the gaps and reflective surfaces of the wall, sounds and images are presented to the visitor in fragments. The shifting sightlines of the visitor climbing the stairs were used as a design instrument for these wooden objects. These same objects are used as bookshelves on their rear faces.

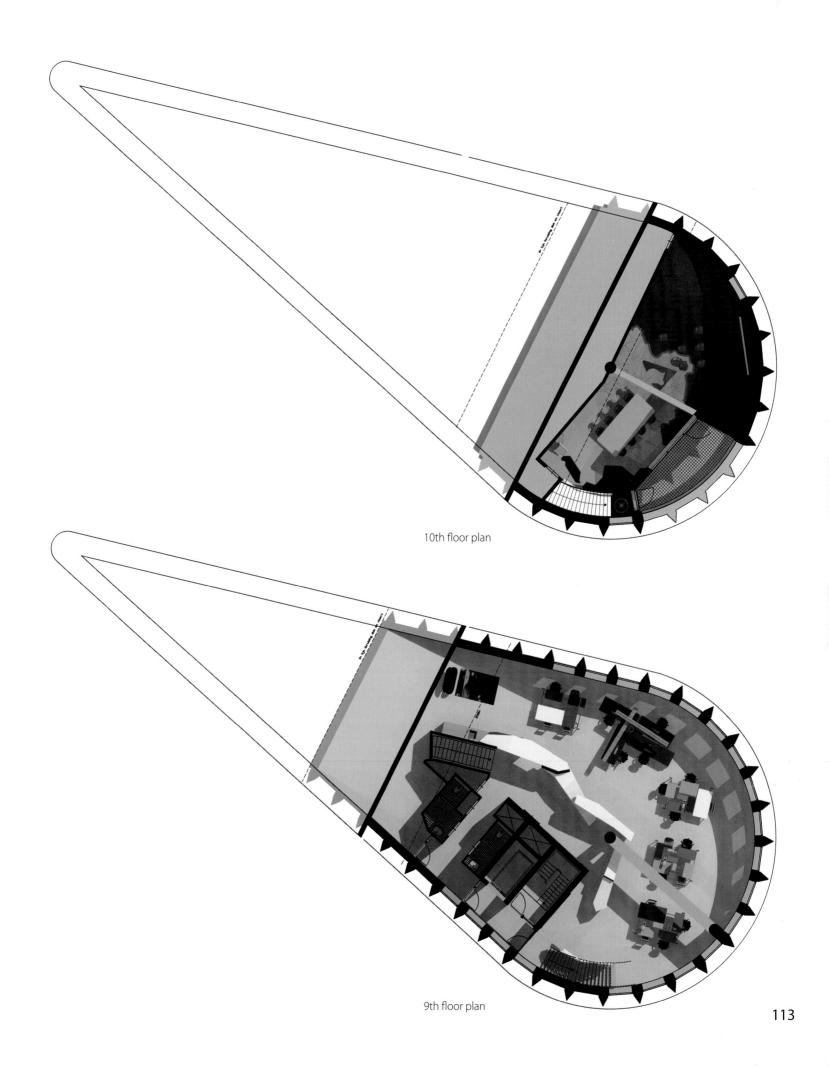

10th floor plan

9th floor plan

113

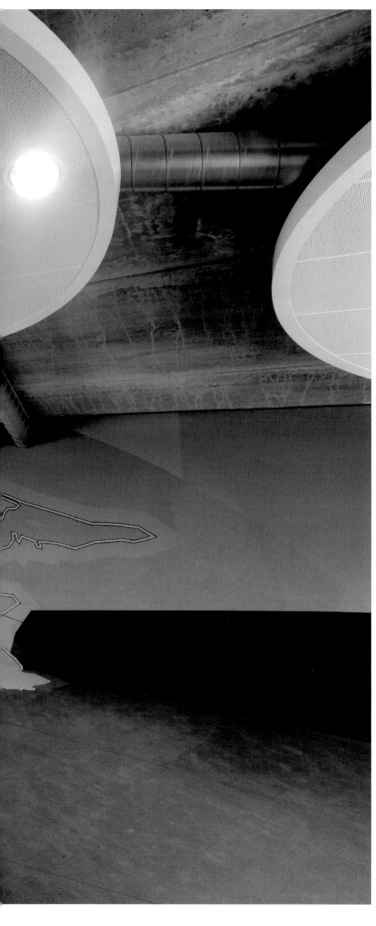

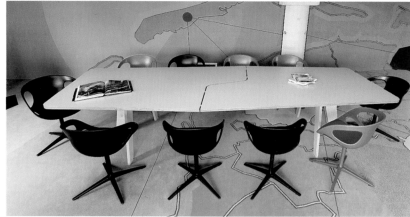

115

Four large tables provide space for sixteen temporary workstations. The tables consist of a steel frame with a tabletop of steel grid panels. The tabletops can be arranged according to each user's needs by combining various desk elements, such as desktops of several sizes, storage objects, book displays and multiple sockets.

117

Nendo

Meguro Offices

Tokyo, Japan

Photographs: Daici Ano

The Japanese headquarters of the Nendo architectural firm are located near the Meguro River in Tokyo on the fifth floor of an old office building. The firm wanted the usual spaces and functions -meeting space, management, workspace and storage- to be separated from one another while at the same time maintaining a sense of connection between them. To achieve this effect, the architects divided the space with walls that seem to sag and flop like a piece of cloth held up between two hands. The various spaces are thus enclosed to a greater extent than they would be by the usual office dividers, but less so than by actual walls.

Employees can move between spaces by walking over the parts of the walls that "sag" the most, thus emphasizing the contrast between the uses of the different spaces. Spaces that need more sound-proofing are enclosed with the kind of plastic curtains you might find at a small factory so that people can work without worrying about noise but not feel isolated. When you stand up and look through the whole space, people, shelves and plants seem to appear and disappear as though floating between the waves. Indeed, fluidity, both visually and physically, combined with tactful respect for the various spaces are key features to the design. People are able to move freely from one space to another while having the capacity to tell at a glance whether they are intruding or not in any given area. Adding to the office's flexibility, furthermore, the wooden panels are not permanent but can be rearranged or removed at any time. In fact, Nendo's designer, Oki Sato, considers these panels to be closer to furniture than to pillars or walls or part of the building's structure.

Architecture:
Nendo

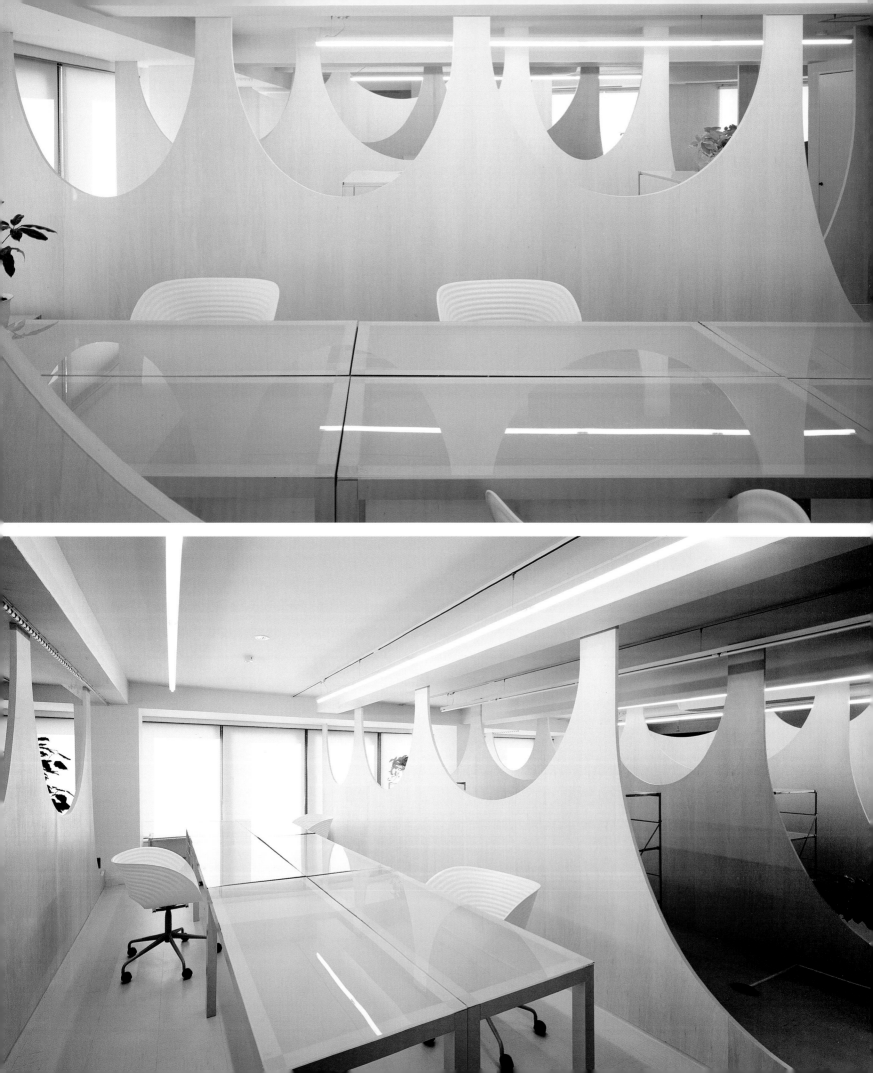

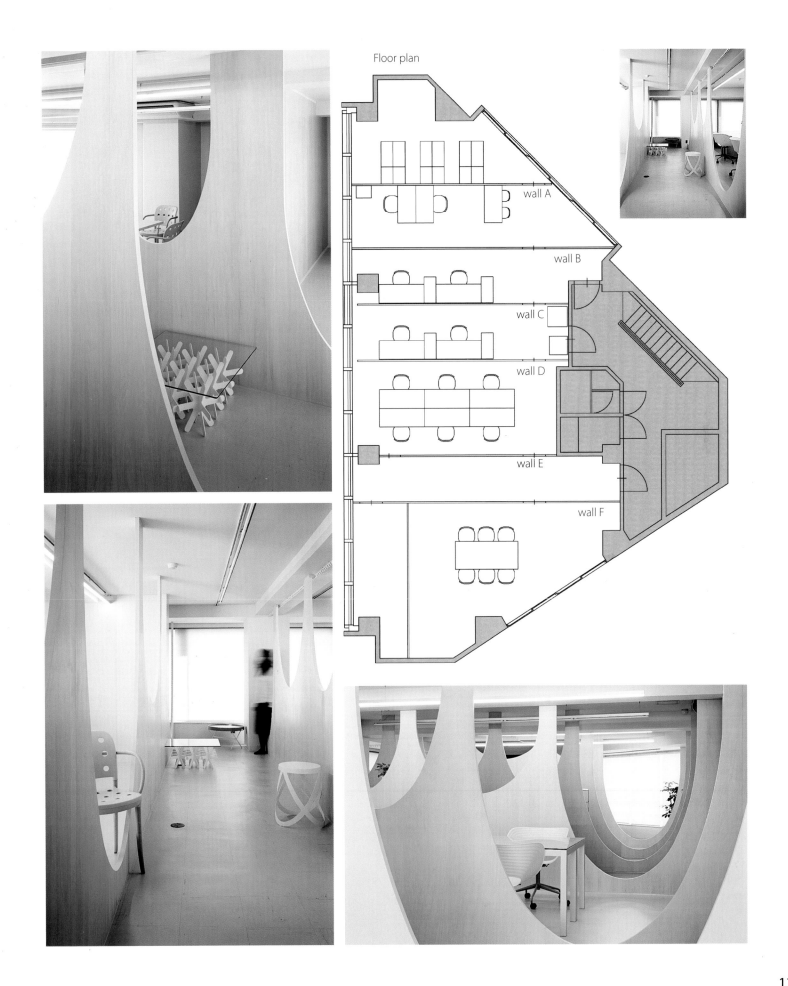

Floor plan

wall A

wall B

wall C

wall D

wall E

wall F

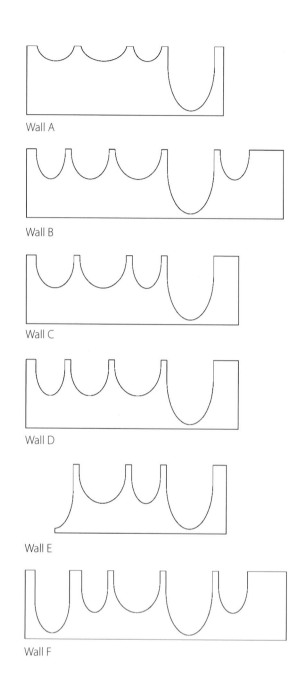

Wall A

Wall B

Wall C

Wall D

Wall E

Wall F

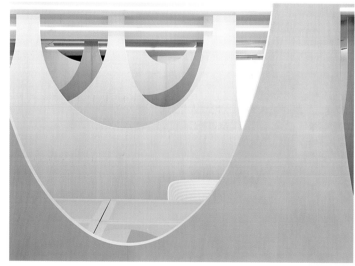

Taranta Creations

Red Town Offices

Red Town Sculpture Park, Shanghai, China

Photographs: Shen Qiang from Shen Photo

Shanghai based practice Taranta Creations has designed their own studio in Shanghai, China. The design is a reflection of the ongoing creative process within the studio. The intervention seeks to provide an adaptable space that supports a range of informal functions.

The office is situated in a former metal factory. The distance between the existing steel structure and ceiling was too small to fit a much-needed second floor into the space. The architects resolved the problem by creating a horizontal surface just above the steel structure with four workstations placed in the space between the steel sections. This way the "floor" is transformed into one continuous desk, while the four recessed stations provide a more traditional workspace. The large 'work floor' invites the designers to use the open space for thinking, sketching, meeting, drafting, modeling, sitting and relaxing. This informal interpretation of office space encourages cross-pollination between the different projects and disciplines occurring within the studio.

On the lower floor the individual workstations are placed by the windows. A green sculptural table can be used for communal activities. Informal and contoured, the central staircase is reminiscent of a large droplet of water ready to fall from the ceiling. Inside the stairwell, a highly saturated environment of bright red engulfs and surrounds the individual, dramatically marking the transition between the different office areas. The color is repeated on the second floor as an accent to highlight the recessed work areas.

Architecture:
Taranta Creations
Design team:
Enrico Taranta,
Giorgio Radojkovic,
Juriaan Calis
Built area:
120 sqm (1,290 sqft)

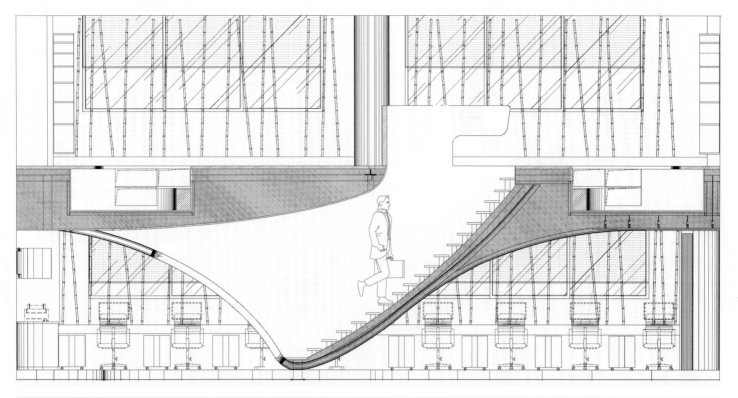

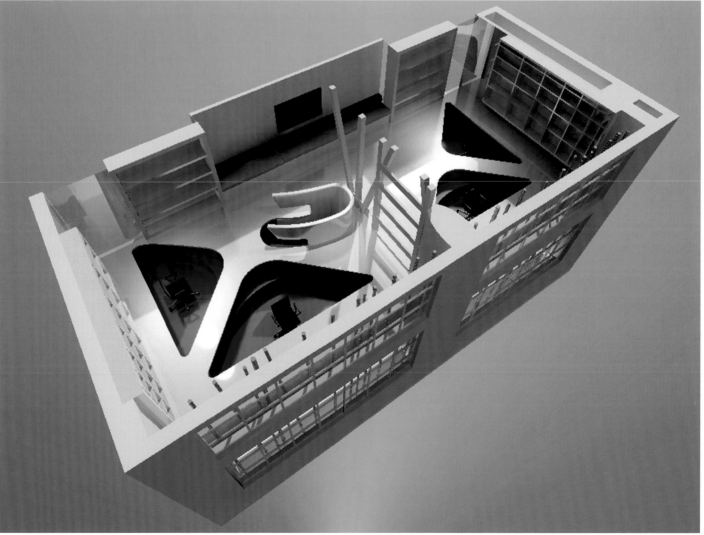

Facet Studio

Studio Spec

Sydney, Australia

Photographs: Katherine Lu

Three functions, two characters, one irregular office space: this demanding project cleverly integrates three separate programs – a graphic design studio, a graphic design school and a beauty consultation room – by creating spaces within the main space through the installation of two opposed wooden boxes. The existing room was characterized by a combination of white walls, white ceiling and black-framed windows; it was basically a monotone space.

The clients are a husband and wife. He runs a graphic design business while she operates a beauty consultancy. Thankfully, the clients' favorite colors are black and white respectively. Hence, the designers proposed a simple box with a black interior for the husband and one with a white interior for the wife. The exterior colors of the boxes are the inverse of the interior colors. Thus, the alternating repetition of black, white, black, white emerges when looking from the husband's workplace into the wife's. Likewise, one perceives a repetition of white, black, white, black from the opposite end; this dynamic rhythm creates a sense of motion. The dynamic rhythm is intended to provide for an active and productive working environment for the people who work within this space. The monotone elements of the studio are set off by the rich warm tone of the varnished timber floorboards.

Architecture:
Facet Studio

Design team:
Olivia Shih, Yoshihito Kashiwagi

Main material:
Timber

Surface area:
75 sqm (810 sqft)

FLOOR PLAN

1. Entry
2. Reception
3. Beauty salon
4. Graphic design studio
5. Server room
6. Kitchen
7. Class room 2
8. Work room
9. Class room 1

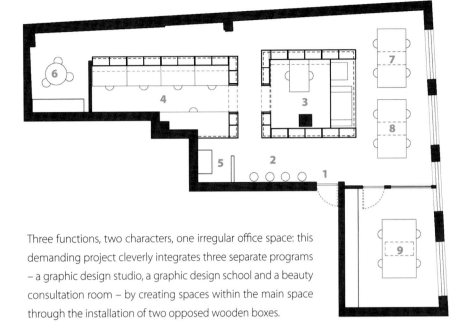

Three functions, two characters, one irregular office space: this demanding project cleverly integrates three separate programs – a graphic design studio, a graphic design school and a beauty consultation room – by creating spaces within the main space through the installation of two opposed wooden boxes.

Essentia Designs Limited

Dentsu London

London, UK

Photographs: contributed by Essentia Designs Limited

Essentia Designs were approached through project managers Interactive Space to work on the offices for Dentsu London, a creative agency based in the UK. The offices are located in a building in an award winning development by Amanda Levete which the Dentsu team have already christened the "spaceship". The brief was to create a high-tech Japanese minimalist interior that would be in keeping with the curvaceous exterior of the building. In addition to the main agency studio spaces and the European head office, the brief included working space for Attik, an associated multi-award winning branding agency.

The decision to relocate Attik in London meant the solution needed to encourage integration and cross-fertilisation between the two businesses. In addition, the European headquarters team were moving from separate offices in Mayfair so this would be the first opportunity for the business to function out of a single location.

From a strategic perspective, the top floor penthouse was ideal for the boardroom. The main reception area was located on the 5th floor to simplify the client journey and provide space for Dentsu Europe. The 4th floor was retained as the main creative studio hub, while Attik have their own space on the third floor, which includes an exhibition space and padded meeting room, along with a shared canteen and library space. The decision to locate these shared facilities adjacent to the Attik team was to encourage social engagement and speed up integration of the businesses.

The scheme took inspiration from sources as disparate as Star Trek, Spitfire fighter planes, Buckminster Fuller and Eriko Horiki's paper sculptures. The color pallet of whites and grays is lightened by the vibrant green used in the floor finishes of the building's common areas. The existing building is highly energy efficient and uses a chilled beam AC system with integral low energy lighting, so an open plan, agile layout was chosen for the working space with no closed offices and only the bare minimum of meeting rooms. The 4th floor studio space has freestanding pods for collaborative brainstorming.

The designers wanted to retain as much of the base build elements as possible, so developed the concept of a curved tensile fabric screen to separate the client reception area from the Dentsu Europe team. The reception is entered through a fabric tunnel which peels back to reveal the thermo-formed corian reception desk and client waiting area, a fitting introduction to this amazing agency.

Architecture:
Essentia Designs Limited

Project managers:
Interactive Space

Main contractor:
Virtus Contracts Limited

Flooring:
Versatile Flooring Co

Reception screen:
Tensile Fabrics

System furniture:
Task Systems & Vitra

Loose furniture:
Viaduct

Specialist joinery:
Select Shopfitters

The brief for this office fit-out was to create a high-tech Japanese minimalist interior that would be in keeping with the curvaceous exterior of the building. In addition to the studio spaces and European headquarters of Dentsu London, the brief included working space for Attik, an associated multi-award winning branding agency.

Floor plan

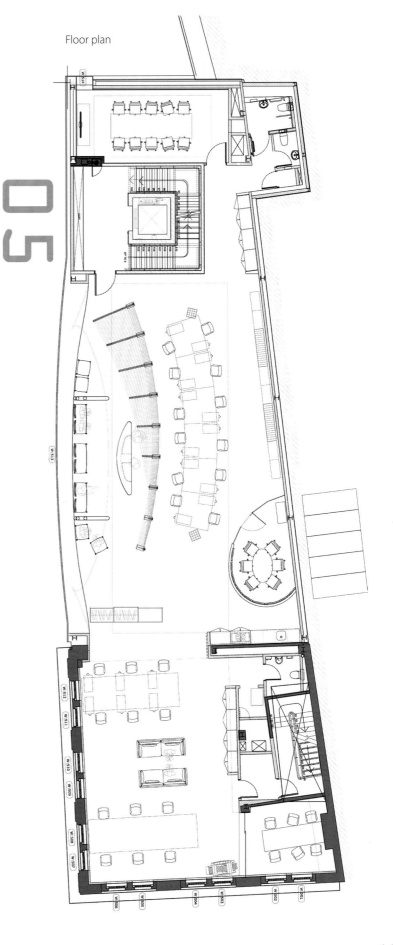

Studio SKLIM

Thin Office

Jalan Besar, Singapore

Photographs: Jeremy San, Studio SKLIM

While tapping on a laptop in a café has become the ubiquitous platform to begin "work", the need for a permanent work environment for any office is still necessary in the long run. Perhaps what has changed since the advent of "coffee offices" has been the increasing need for flexibility within a sedentary work sphere.

The program brief was for an office space shared by two companies, an IT company and a multi-media setup. Located in a refurbished post-war building in Singapore's CBD outskirts, the space was long and narrow with split levels, offering the possibility of a raised space. Throughout the long and narrow office, the ceiling and wall conditions were left unaltered as much as possible, along with the existing light fixtures.

The designed space was to reflect the ethos of the companies: flexibility, technology and creativity. The office space was loosely organised into eight clusters, namely: the Boss Boxes, Long Work Top, Discussion Table, Welcome Mat, Sanitary & Storage, Recharging Point, Twist Platform and Multi-media Corner. Each of these clusters was arranged around an open plan configuration, with the exception of Sanitary & Storage, to allow a multifarious overlap of working trajectories.

The flexible working environment was kept in mind with the possibility of hot-desking, informal working clusters and also semi-private cubicles. The Boss Boxes were an option for more privacy as some work required a certain level of seclusion. Technology is a crucial aspect of any modern day office and the ease of being "connected" to either an internet network or a power source was one of the concerns of the client.

The fluctuating size of the workforce also meant flexible working spaces which could be contracted and expanded to fit the demands of this office. The result was the "Long Work Top" which incorporated an ingenious power strip of data points, power supply and telecommunication points to be accessible at any location along this table, expanding the number of workstations from 6 to 10 in a few minutes. This single piece of stretched work surface became part of a greater string of furniture transforming from tabletop, reception seating, storage and finally to pantry space.

Architecture:
Studio SKLIM

Client:
Kido Technologies

Key personnel:
Kevin Lim

Floor area:
120 sqm (1,292 sqft)

146

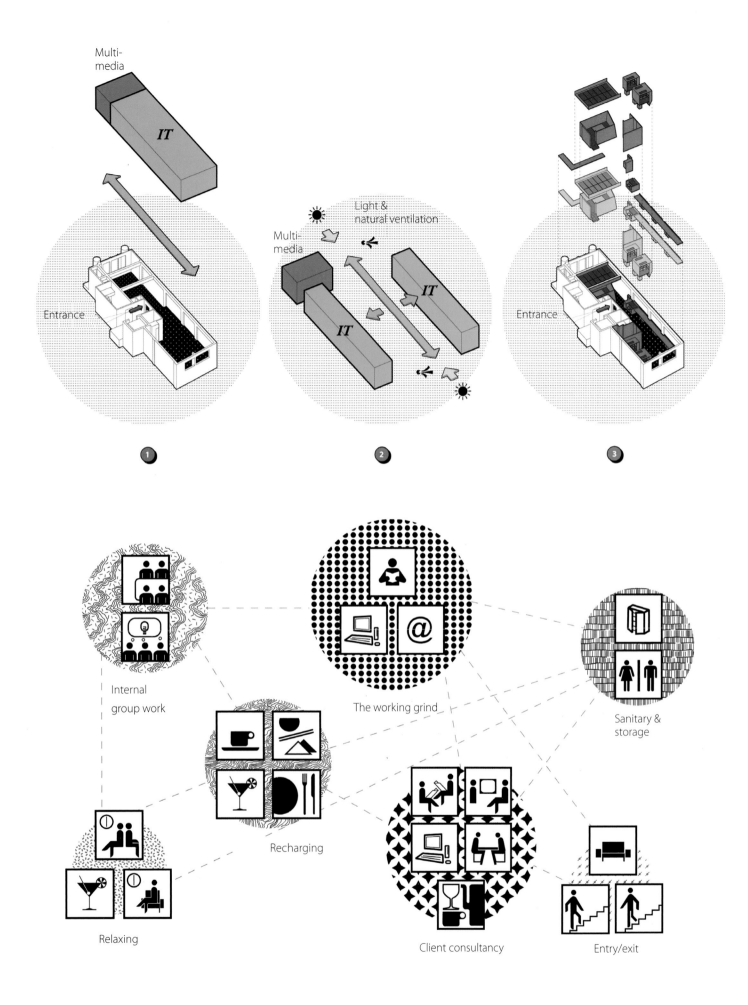

Multi-media

IT

Entrance

1

Light &
natural ventilation

Multi-media

IT

IT

2

Entrance

3

Internal
group work

The working grind

Sanitary &
storage

Recharging

Relaxing

Client consultancy

Entry/exit

149

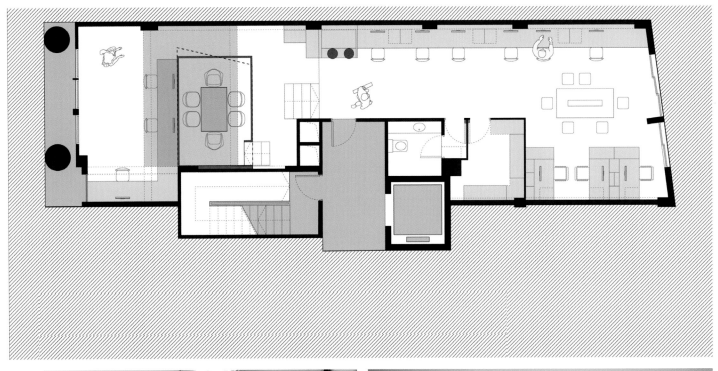

The unconventional form of the Twist Platform in an otherwise sleek and straightforward office space added a dynamic backdrop to the Recharging Point and provided privacy to the independent operation of the multi-media setup. The giant overhead light fixture was a final touch to the suggestion of this event space.

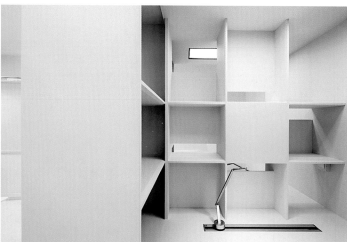

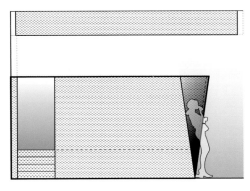

Front elevation

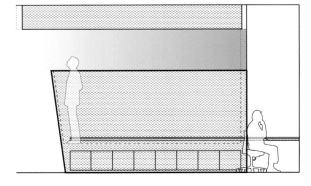

Back elevation

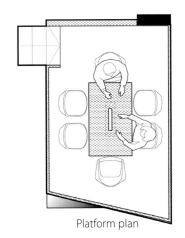

Platform plan

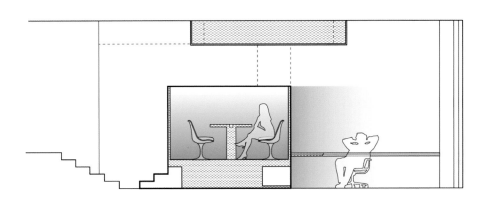

Longitudinal section

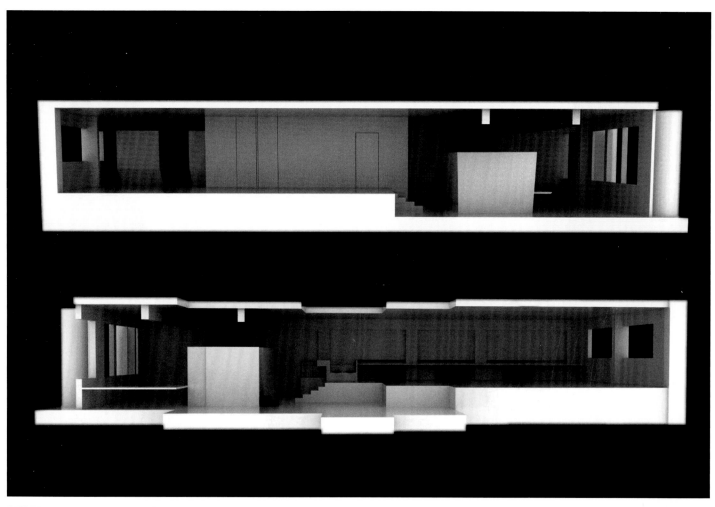

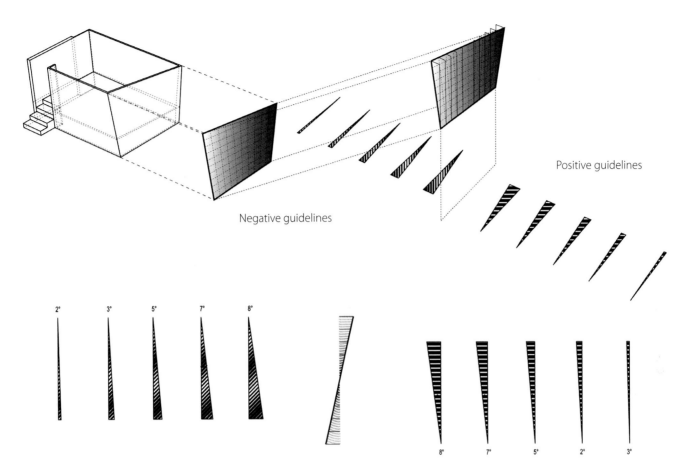

Negative guidelines

Positive guidelines

2° 3° 5° 7° 8°

8° 7° 5° 2° 3°

The essence of this "Thin Office" is a desire to remain anonymous and to provide a blank canvas for various work scenarios and possibilities. This "thinness" is translated from the basic organisation of spaces which open up a central thoroughfare for circulation, light and natural ventilation, through to the furniture details which celebrate the geometrical state of being folded, suspended or twisted.

Bottega + Ehrhardt Architekten

Publicmotor Brand Communication

Stuttgart, Germany

Photographs: David Franck Photographie

A loft space with an overall size of about 700 sqm in the center of Stuttgart was transformed into the new office space for PUBLICMOTOR.

One enters the office by passing through a "forest" of triangular, dark gray volumes, to an open space and the waiting area, defined by a golden circle on the white floor. Small LCD screens are integrated into the back of the triangular volumes, showing projects and works by the agency. Rectangular volumes covered with a light gray carpet divide the space into separate workstations. The volumes serve as cupboards, acoustic insulation and have integrated lighting. The management workstations and the meeting room are divided by floor to ceiling glass partitions and their degree of privacy can be individually controlled with bronze-colored semitransparent curtains.

Yellow vertical volumes, serving as the office library, separate the working area from the communication zone. A long wooden table, where the office comes together for lunch, is connected to a small kitchen in the back of the space. Behind a carpet-covered wall, the service zone contains the cutting rooms of the agency and the toilets. A continuous white polyurethane floor emphasizes the openness of the space.

Architecture:
Bottega + Ehrhardt Architekten

Project architect:
Christoph Seebald

Client:
Publicmotor GmbH

Floor area:
700 sqm (7,530 sqft)

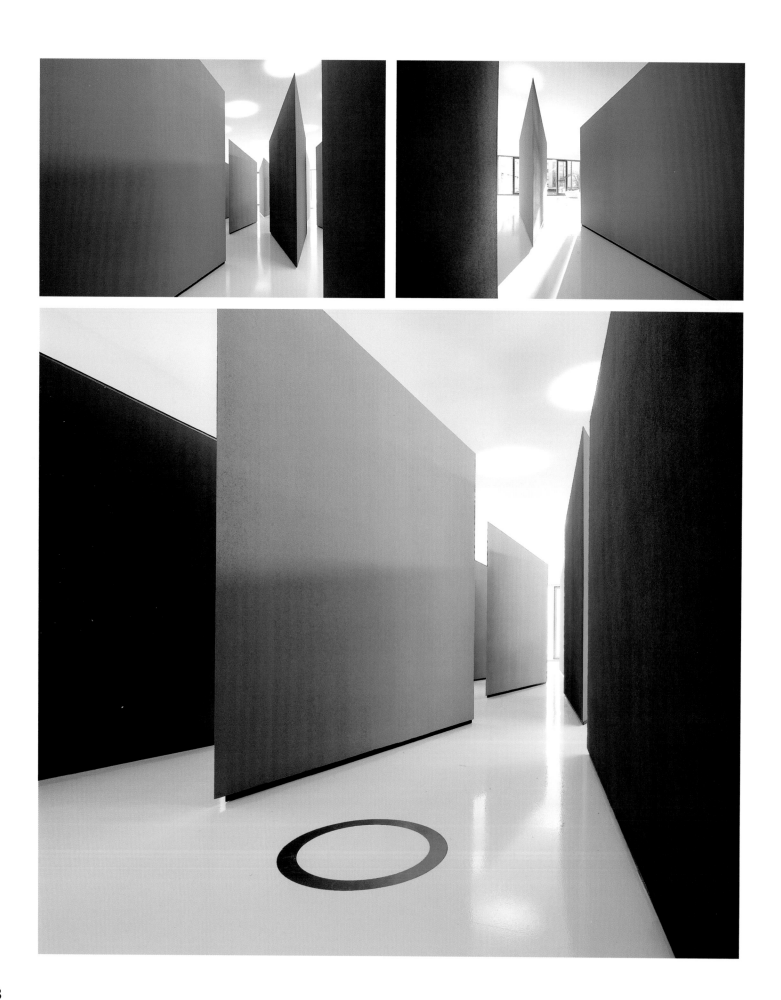

Floor plan

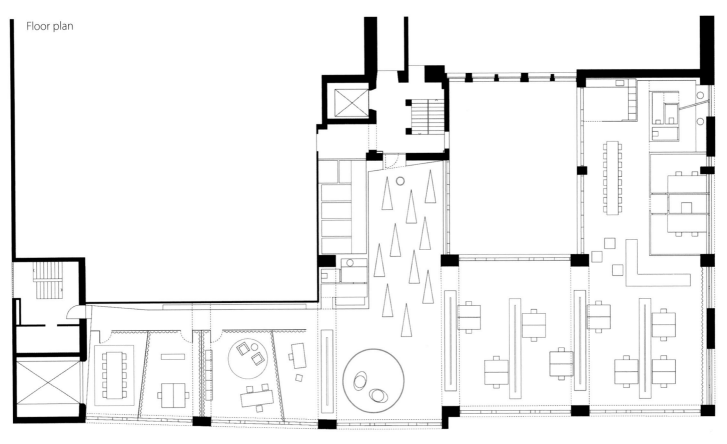

The management workstations and the meeting room are divided by floor to ceiling glass partitions and their degree of privacy can be individually controlled with bronze-colored semitransparent curtains.

Jackie-B

Cubion a/s Offices

Copenhagen, Denmark

Photographs: Cubion a/s | Jacob Nielsen

Located in the heart of Copenhagen, the consultant company Cubion a/s occupies the lower floor of a listed house dating from 1793. The house is on one of the principal pedestrian streets in the oldest part of Copenhagen.

Cubion a/s decided in 2007 to move their Copenhagen office into new surroundings. They contacted the Danish designer Jackie-B and asked him to create a creative oasis where customers would find a place for inspiration and understanding and a place where solutions were designed, rethought and questioned.

Jackie-B took the challenge and turned the office into three different rooms for the exchange of knowledge and conversation with the design emphasis on simplicity of both forms and color.

The main office houses workstations for eight employees on two groups of green tables. The office is lit by suspended light fittings custom designed for the room by Jackie-B. The office walls are decorated with synthetic grass islands that can be leant on and help to generate a dreamy and calm atmosphere. The glass wall at the entrance to the office has a bubble diagram for brainstorming etched upon it to be used as a whiteboard.

The kitchen is designed as a social meeting room with a bright yellow table that centers the room. A forest of Photostats leads into the back office where a representation of a child's playhouse with small lamp flowers stands as a shining white homage to play and imagination. The sofa house offers space for deep thoughts and loose conversations. The back office also contains external work points so employers can retrieve documents and work away from the main office.

The office is designed to support and stimulate an environment that gives the employees and customers a new experience of what an office can be.

Architecture:
Jackie-B

Floor area:
178 sqm (1,920 sqft)

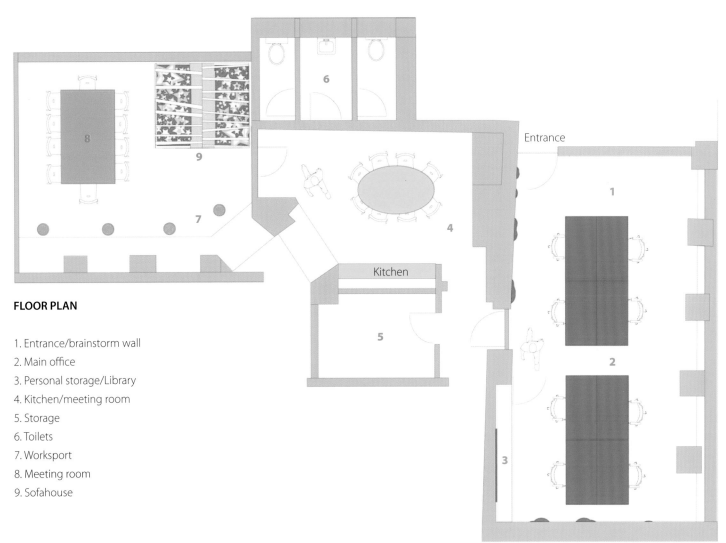

FLOOR PLAN

1. Entrance/brainstorm wall
2. Main office
3. Personal storage/Library
4. Kitchen/meeting room
5. Storage
6. Toilets
7. Worksport
8. Meeting room
9. Sofahouse

Entrance

Kitchen

A forest of Photostats leads into the back office where a representation of a child's playhouse with small lamp flowers stands as a shining white homage to play and imagination. The sofa house offers space for deep thoughts and loose conversations.

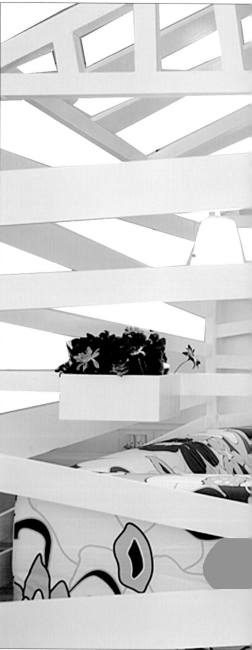

The main office houses workstations for eight employees on two groups of green tables. The suspended light fittings have been custom designed by Jackie-B. The office walls are decorated with synthetic grass islands that can be leant on and help to generate a dreamy and calm atmosphere.

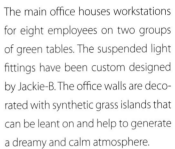

The office is designed to support and stimulate an environment that gives the employees and customers a new experience of what an office can be.

Abeijón-Fernández

MAXAN

A Coruña, Spain

Photographs: Santos-Díez

The architects were commissioned by the advertising company Maxan to design the firm's offices in A Coruña. The goal was to create a workplace in which the company's business philosophy was always present; an office, in short, that reflected the firm's personality.

The office is located one flight above street level and its connection to the street is a black stairway designed to contrast with the white, neutral space of the interior.

The concept of the space is open; the different departments interrelate visually and spatially with one another, following the work method of the firm. Divisions are kept to a minimum and if they exist, tend to dematerialise through the use of glass.

False ceilings, emphasized through the use of indirect light, and furnishings have been used as configuring elements for the spaces, achieving a high level of interior permeability. Custom-made furnishings were made by Distecar S.L, with chairs by Arper.

The purity of the white space is interrupted through the use of colours representative of the company; these appear in the zones destined for dealing with clients. Work by the advertising company is placed in different spaces throughout the office to form part of the dialogue established between the interior design and the firm's activity.

The office has façades on two streets, thus, in order to ensure a unified reading of the space, black horizontal strips have been placed that control the entrance of light into the interior of the premises while at the same time serving as a support for the company's logotype.

Architecture:
Abeijón-Fernández
(José Abeijón Vela, Miguel Fernández Carreiras)

Client:
Maxan

Contractors:
Grupo Tecam

Custom furnishings:
Distecar S.L.

Floor area:
632 sqm (6,803 sqft)

QUEREMOS QUE ENAMORES. QUEREMOS QUE
LA GENTE TE MIRE Y TE DESEE, QUE EL MUNDO
SE DETENGA CUANDO APAREZCAS. AUNQUE SEAS
GUAPO, INTELIGENTE E INGENIOSO,
PUEDES TENER UN CARISMA EXCEPCIONAL,
SI NO ENAMORAS, NO EXISTES.

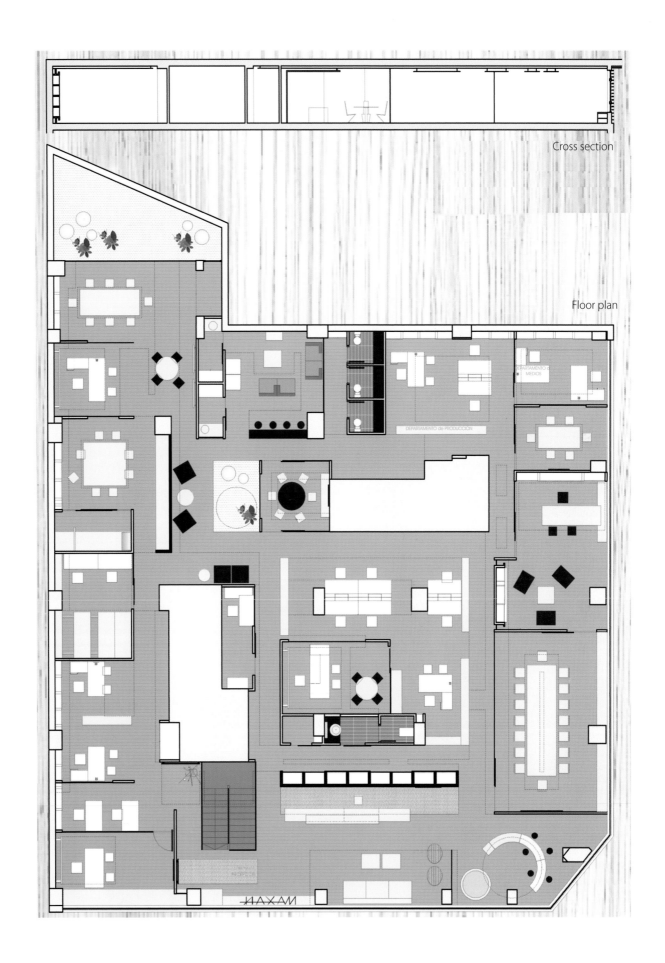

Cross section

Floor plan

178

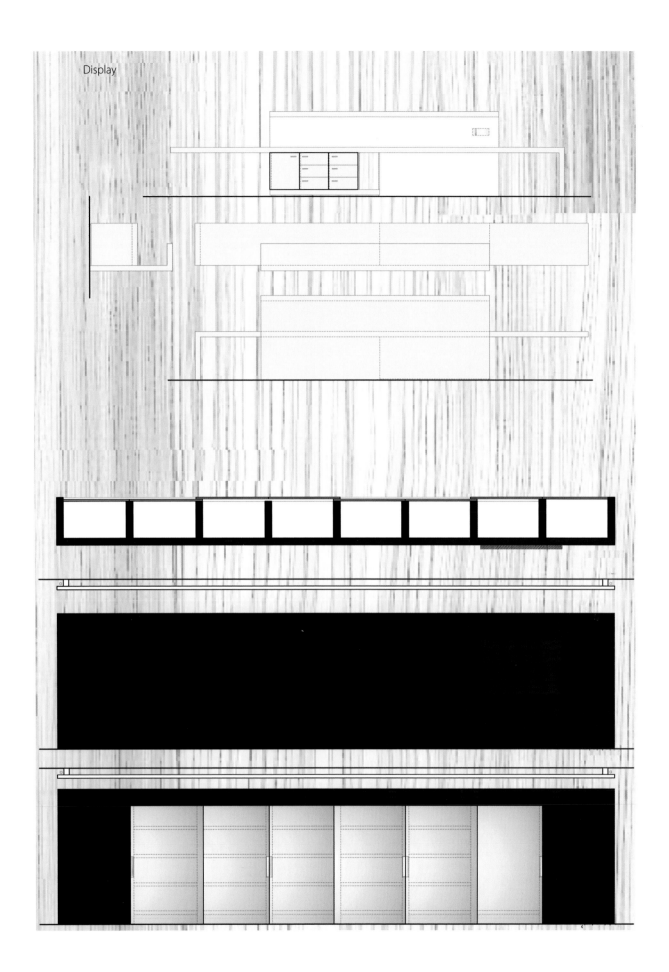

Display

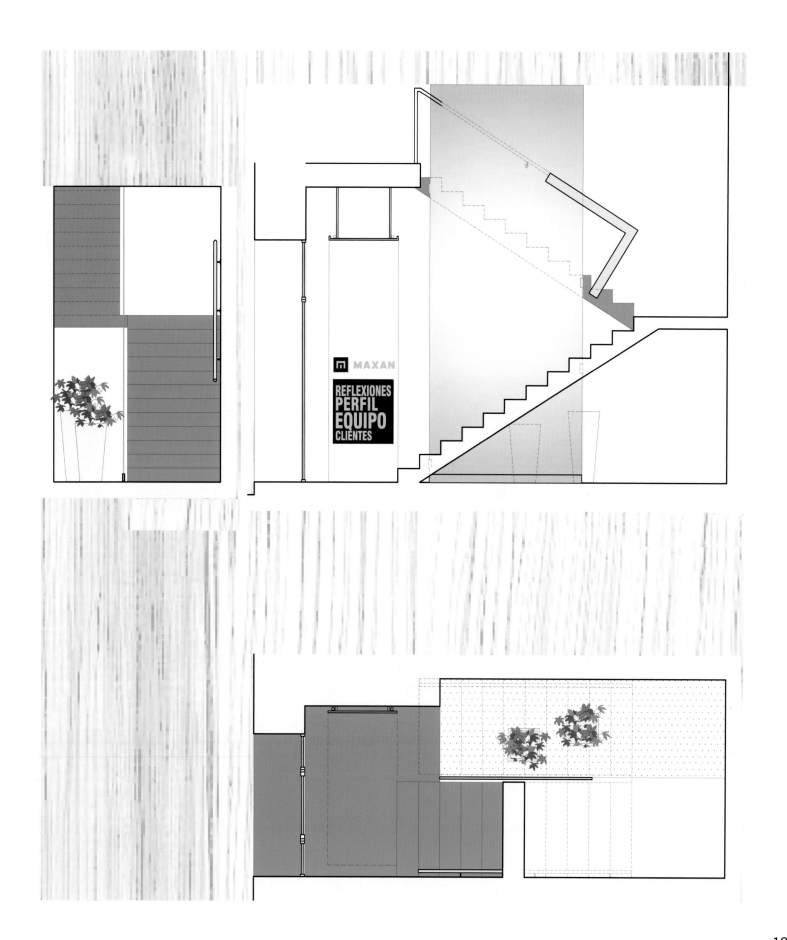

REFLEXIONES
PERFIL
EQUIPO
CLIÈNTES

N59 architects

Kapero Offices

Stockholm, Sweden

Photographs: Peter Rutherhagen

This striking fit-out for the Kapero consultants offices in Stockholm is defined by two features: the color scheme – white with canary yellow highlights – and an arrow motif which represents the firm's consulting activities. Custom made white lacquered MDF furniture pieces separate the functional zones of the office: the service area behind the reception desk, a creative area for group work and the workstations zone. The heights of the furniture pieces vary between 90 and 210 centimeters to create different degrees of transparency or privacy between the different zones, while 80 cm high yellow cabinets separate the individual workstations but are sufficiently low to allow spontaneous communication.

Heavy sliding glass doors fitted with a canary yellow film separate the meeting room and coffee area from the open-plan working area. While the mass of the glass doors acts as acoustic insulation between these areas and the rest of the office, the acoustic absorbency of the spaces is increased with off-white carpeting.

The CNC-milled arrows that adorn all areas of the office are more than just aesthetic spice – they also serve as cabinet handles in the furniture pieces and as vents in the heating covers. The rawness of the ceiling with its exposed structure and service ducts contrasts with the polished perfection of the shiny white epoxy resin floor. The waiting / lounge area is distinguished by Eames chairs.

Architecture:
N59 architects
Floor area:
192 sqm (2,100 sqft)

This striking fit-out for the Kapero consultants offices in Stockholm is defined by two features: the color scheme – white with canary yellow highlights – and an arrow motif which represents the firm's consulting activities. The CNC-milled arrows that adorn all areas of the office are more than just aesthetic spice – they also serve as cabinet handles in the furniture pieces and as vents in the heating covers.

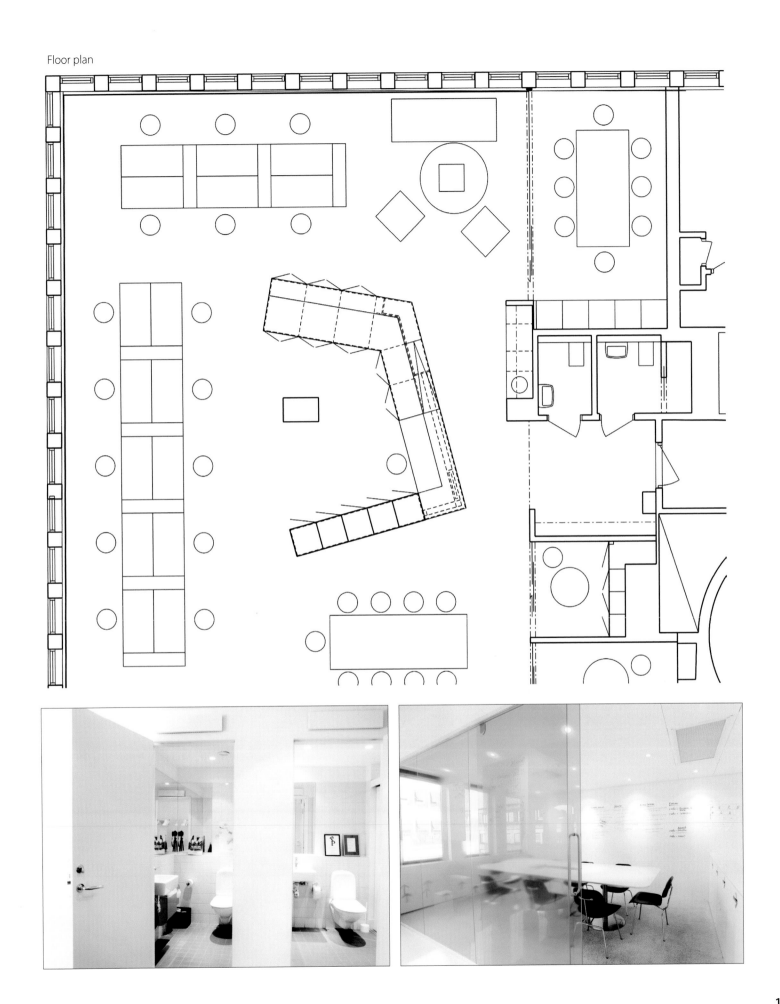

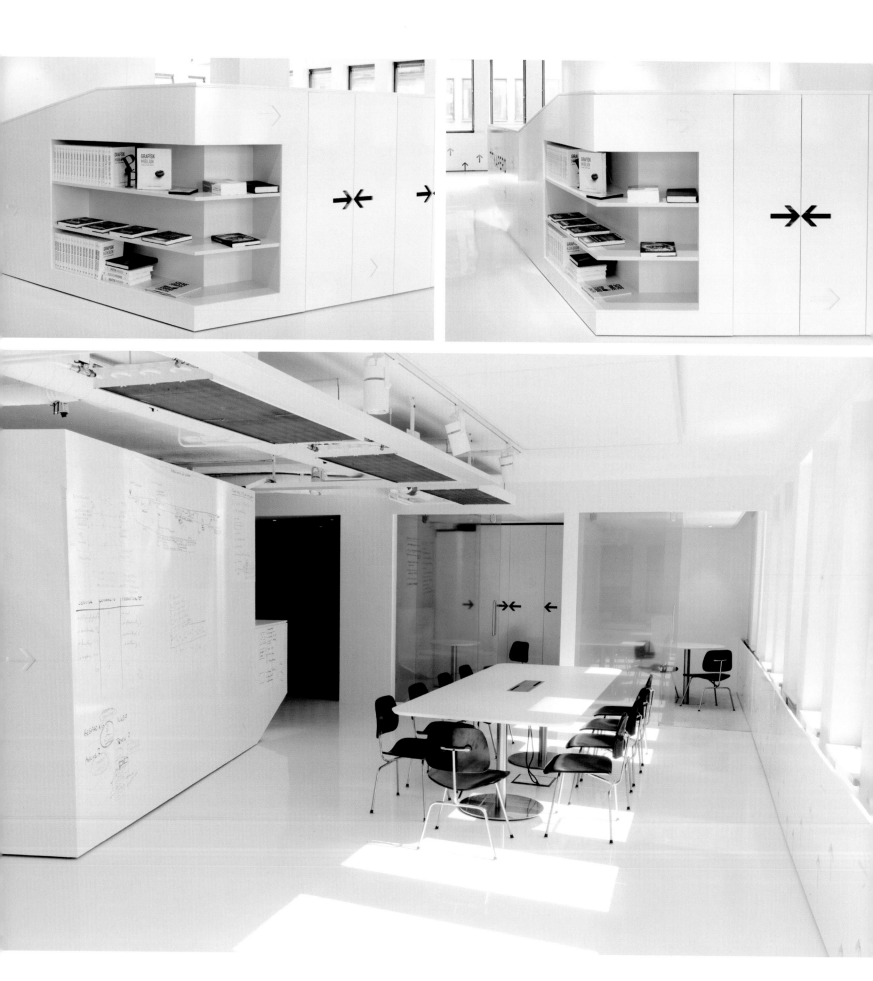

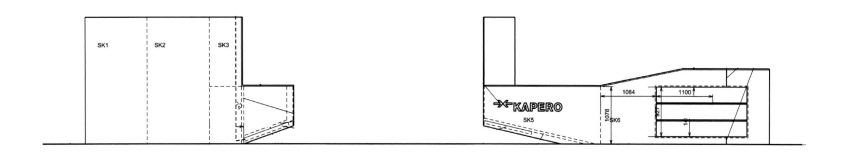

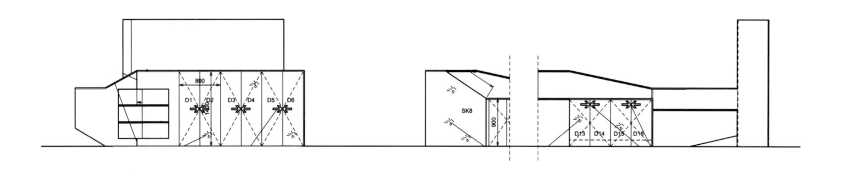

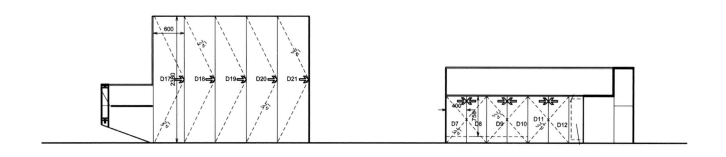

GPAC

Saegeling Medizintechnik

Heidenau, Germany

Photographs: Gunter Binsack

German architects Gerd Priebe Architects & Consultants (GPAC) designed a new office building for medical equipment developers, Saegeling Medizintechnik, situated in the company's existing complex. The curved shape of the two-storey building has been designed to fit in among the neighbouring, low-rise buildings and surrounding environment. The firm was awarded the German certificate for sustainable buildings (German Sustainable Building Council – DGNB).

Based on the existing small scale building structures in the vicinity, the studio of GPAC designed an elegantly curved two-story building structure that despite is deliberately unique form fits harmoniously into the existing urban fabric. Sustainability was taken into account from the start of planning and played an integral part in the design. Integral planning, user comfort, visual comfort, acoustic comfort and thermal comfort were all carefully incorporated.

The spacious and open character of the new building manifests itself on the east side where the curving glass façade envelopes a secluded outdoor space which visually flows into the indoor space. The glass façade dominates and communicates a heightened sense of openness and light-flooded space. Two functional areas divide the building. To the south, the reception area or public space welcomes visitors and leads them through a two-storey lobby that doubles as an events space. Adjoining the area on the ground floor is a meeting room for clients, while a gallery is located on the upper floor. The internal functions are situated on the building's north side. Here, individual office space as well as a copy room and a generous open office area are integrated into the design.

In configuring an effective office and work area, the strict partitioning of user and circulation space was discarded with the aim of creating a flowing, efficient and practically support-free architecture. Internal office processes are mirrored in the building's structure in the form of optimized workstations, short communication and circulation paths, as well as established visual relationships between the interior and exterior of the building. The efficiently designed office units in turn enabled the expansive configuration of the public spaces.

Architecture:
Gerd Priebe Architects & Consultants (GPAC)

192

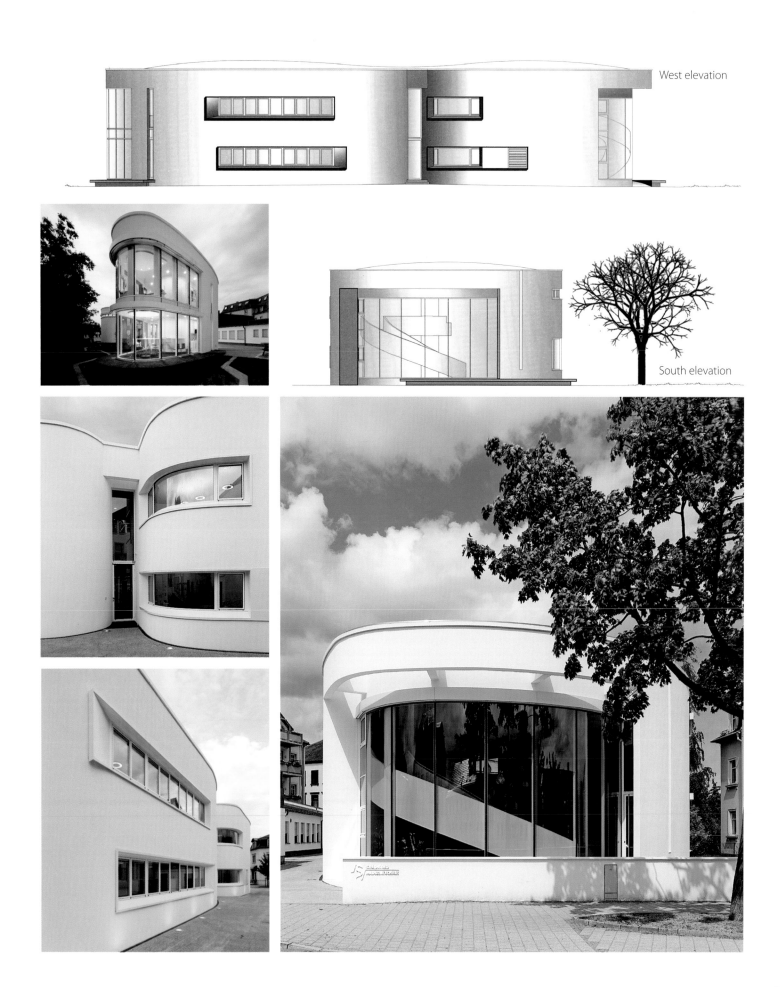

West elevation

South elevation

193

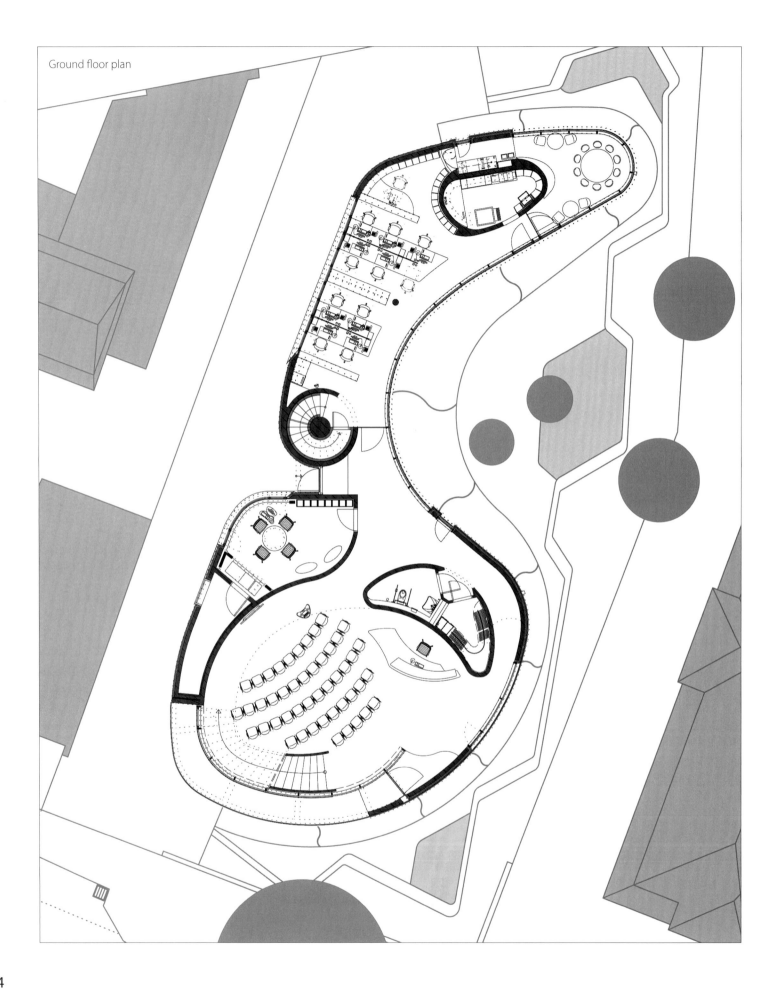

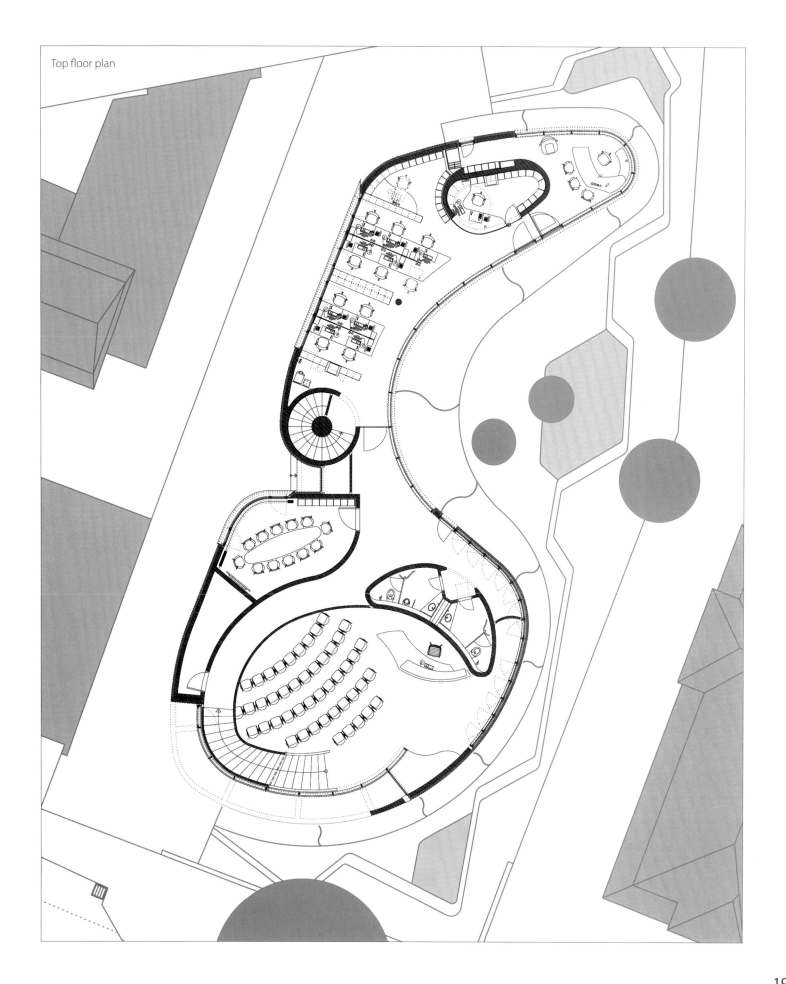

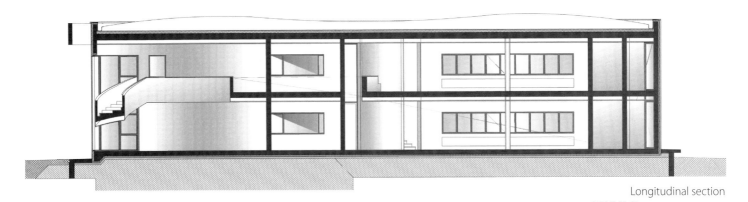

Longitudinal section

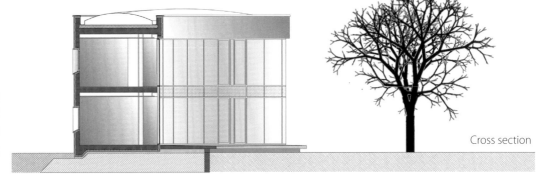

Cross section

The curvilinear shape of the building optimizes the rigidity and stability of the load-bearing construction and allows for a reduction in materials and wall thicknesses.

COEN!

Besturenraad / BKO Offices

Woerden, the Netherlands

Photographs: COEN! | Roy van de Meulengraaf

COEN! created a new working environment and identity layer for Besturenraad and BKO – the dutch education boards which run, respectively, the Protestant and Catholic faith schools in the Netherlands. These two organizations have moved into joint premises in order to work together in a cooperative structure in achieving what are effectively common goals. The aim of this project was to visually connect the shared goals and principles of both organizations.

For the design narrative of the project, COEN! used "the book" as a metaphor. Aside from its importance in the Protestant and Catholic faiths, a book also consists of structure, text and images. The decorative elements used in the interior design include stained glass patterns, metal grids with patterns based on the golden section and printed text. The relationship between faith and education is represented by DNA patterns and golden 'office altars'.

In the modern age a new "religion" has developed from a belief in the global economy, in which Materialism has usurped the role of God. As this vacuous system of values drives people to redouble their search for new forms of spiritual enrichment, space is also created for new types of religious experiences and spirituality. This search for new meaning leads ultimately to inner reflection. The tension that exists between the material and the spiritual was the inspiration for the logo called 'Faithless' designed by Coen van Ham for the new headquarters, a piece of art based on an inversion of material and void to reflect the dichotomy between the spiritual and the material.

Architecture:
COEN! design agency

Client:
Besturenraad / BKO, Woerden

Interior architect:
COEN! design agency

Interior builder:
De Vastgoedinrichter and
Gielissen interiors & exhibitions

Floor area:
2,200 sqm (23,700 sqft)

First floor plan

Ground floor plan

Colorful DNA patterns on the walls in the offices give all spaces their unique appearance

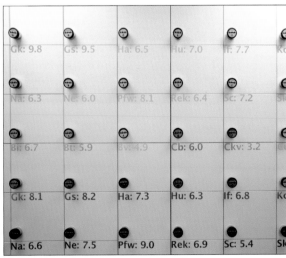

Gk: 9.8	Gs: 9.5	Ha: 6.5	Hu: 7.0	If: 7.7	Kc
Na: 6.3	Ne: 6.0	Pfw: 8.1	Rek: 6.4	Sc: 7.2	Sk
Bt: 6.7	Bt: 5.9	Bvo: 4.9	Cb: 6.0	Ckv: 3.2	Cu
Gk: 8.1	Gs: 8.2	Ha: 7.3	Hu: 6.3	If: 6.8	Kc
Na: 6.6	Ne: 7.5	Pfw: 9.0	Rek: 6.9	Sc: 5.4	Sk

Bates Smart Architects

Media House

Melbourne, Australia   **Photographs:** contributed by Bates Smart Architects

Bates Smart's new 5-star Green Star and 4.5 star NABERS rated building showcases The Age as a leading media organisation and a great place to work. Through the careful and innovative design of the building and interiors, Media House embraces the 'New Fairfax' that sees the merging of print and digital platforms under one roof.

The design concept was based on the process of the media and how information is perceived and processed. This led to the idea of the virtual and reality, or virtual reality. Translated into the design, perceptions were explored through transparency, pattern and distortion as well as scale, materiality and texture. The idea being that things may not always be as they seem.

The permeability and transparency of the fit out reinforces The Age's connection to the city of Melbourne and its people, with physical access into the public areas of the building as well as transparency into the drama and energy of the newsroom and supporting workspaces throughout the building. The direct line of sight from the street into key areas was designed specifically to convey messages of transparency, honesty and activity. This is visibly the hub where Melbourne's beloved newspaper is created.

Entering the building, the café lies to the left and The Age Gallery to the right. A 100-seat auditorium allows for both public and internal meetings, live presentations and debates. The Age Gallery is an inside-outside space that is stepped to follow the gradient of Collins Street. Overlaid with strongly contrasting colours, bold patterns and warm timbers, the result is undeniably Melbourne. The gallery wall is constructed of punched white metal and uses a pattern of positive and negative shapes to convey a binary code, representing the digital direction of The Age.

The workplace has been designed with an open plan layout to favor teamwork. Having eliminated the false ceilings, most services are exposed as is the underside of the structural slab. This creates a "media studio" atmosphere and allows light to penetrate deep into the plan. The workspace design ensures a high degree of equity, with all work points separated from the windows – nobody 'owns' the windows. The northern face is fully shaded and fitted out as communal space; a linear breakout and reference zone open to all. Colorful staff hubs are located next to the dramatic stairs on every second floor, encouraging migration and collaboration. Workflows formed the basis for the design solution including the unique arrangement of the News Desk of the future, where the design reflects the deadline-focused critical information flows within the news team. Desks arranged in concentric circles focus on a central meeting table from where the management of the news can be orchestrated.

Architecture:
Bates Smart Pty Ltd

East elevation

Collins Street Bridge

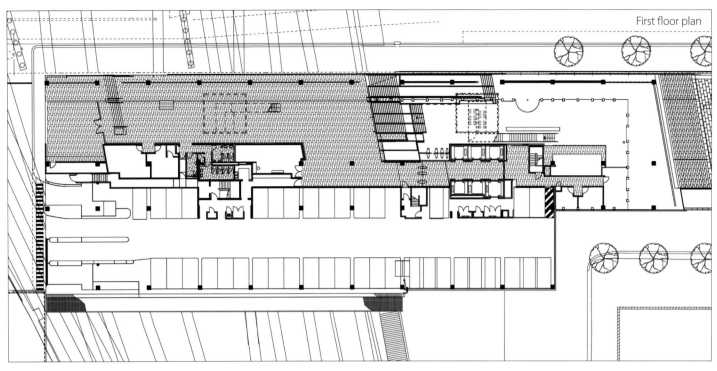

GROUND FLOOR PLAN

	4. Cafe and servery	9. Mail room
	5. Reception	10. Store
1. Piazza lawn	6. Lift lobby	11. Management
2. Outdoor seating	7. Security	12. Kitchen
3. Waiting area	8. Auditorium	13. Entry

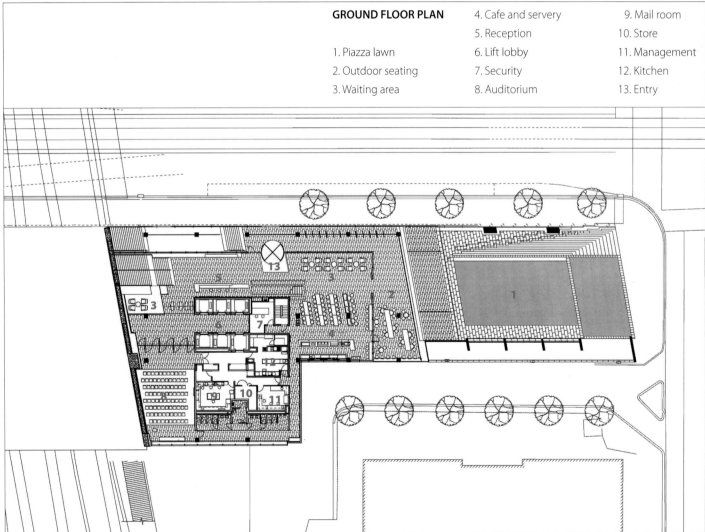

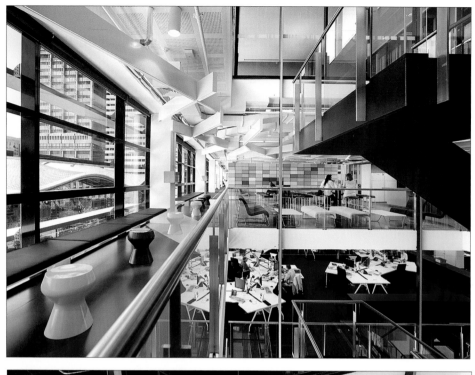

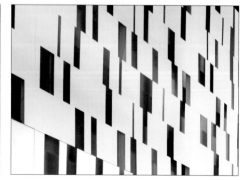

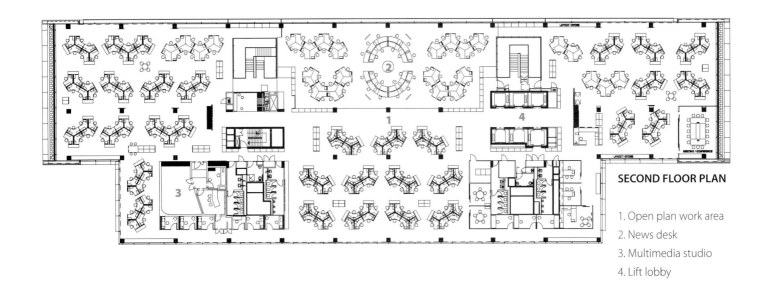

SECOND FLOOR PLAN

1. Open plan work area
2. News desk
3. Multimedia studio
4. Lift lobby

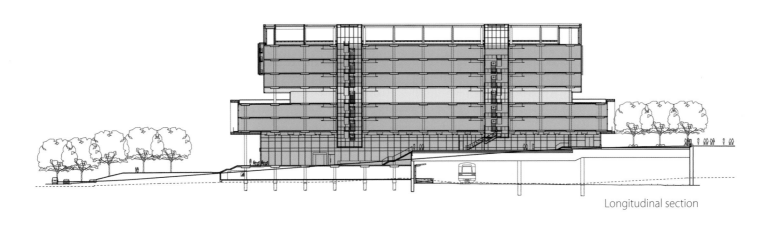

Longitudinal section

215

Elding Oscarson

Oktavilla

Stockholm, Sweden

Photographs: Åke E:son Lindman

This design bureau for magazines and websites is housed in an old textile factory in the center of Stockholm. The client loved the bare, tall and bright spaces, but the building needed to be fully reformed to house the business. There was a mezzanine in the space, with a windowless meeting room underneath and a country style kitchen sprawling along the walls, all arranged in an L-shaped space. The client liked the uninterrupted row of windows, which he wanted to retain. But the program required a bigger meeting room with windows, an atelier table for informal meetings and more workstations, along with an entrance lobby and a small kitchen with a dining table.

Dividing the space with a wall created a large and bright meeting room, as well as a clean rectangular room for the rest of the program. This large space is softly divided with a box containing service functions and a kitchen. By compressing the contents of the box and positioning it carefully, the program effortlessly falls into place without breaking the impression of a single large room. The magnetic galvanized steel cladding picks up the colors of the surroundings in a hazy reflection and defines the box as an inserted element.

The construction of the dividing wall creates the sensation of it being both temporary and solid, while the window inserted within it allows the continuous row of windows in the external wall to be read as a whole. Besides the reference to the client's business, the wall made of stacked bundles of magazines is not only a natural conversation piece, but also works as an acoustic absorbent.

The lighting solution and interior design, which uses Elding Oscarson's own furniture designs mixed with vintage pieces and staples already in the client's possession, highlight the nakedness of the space and the raw, largely untreated building fabric. By adding only two clearly defined architectural elements, the client's wish list could be met while keeping the beauty of the industrial atmosphere of the original building.

Architecture:
Elding Oscarson

Structural engineer:
Konkret

Builder:
Nils Bengtsson Bygg /
Storskog Bygg & Montage

Floor area:
160 sqm (1,720 sqft)

The main space is gently divided with a box containing service functions and a kitchen. By compressing the contents of the box and positioning it carefully, the program effortlessly falls into place without breaking the impression of a single large room. The magnetic galvanized steel cladding picks up the colors of the surroundings in a hazy reflection and defines the box as an inserted element.

Floor plan

The construction of the dividing wall creates the sensation of it being both temporary and solid, while the window inserted within it allows the continuous row of windows in the external wall to be read as a whole. Besides the reference to the client's business, the wall made of stacked bundles of magazines is not only a natural conversation piece, but also works as an acoustic absorbent.

SUE Architekten

Prayer Rahs

Vienna, Austria

Photographs: Hertha Hurnaus

Architecture:
SUE Architekten

Floor area:
390 sqm (4,198 sqft)

Two notaries joined forces and founded a new office in Vienna with the desire to bring a fresh and contemporary feel to their workplace. Initial discussions were held, aided by the architects, to find the right building. A 390-sqm loft in a former telegraph office was selected: a space that expands from a relatively narrow entrance area into a generous, open loft area.

The plan for the office was honed in numerous meetings with the clients, the goal being a workplace that not only created a communicative climate, but also enabled concentrated and uninterrupted work. The result is a layering of the office structure that maximises the potential of the location: at first a friendly entrance area to receive clients, followed by a general office and working area to provide an intimate and concentrated, while still relaxed, communicative atmosphere.

The focus in the central working area is on communication between staff. Stretched storage furniture separates the working area from the hall and communication zone. On one side there are generous cubicles and a meeting room, on the other side of the hall are seating niches, space for photocopiers and a common working area that is shaped by storage furniture. Small windows from the hall allow glimpses into the working areas. The other side of the hall leads to further individual offices.

The layering between the entrance area and the central working space is additionally supported by varying material and colours. Sand-coloured walls and floor tiling dominate the friendly reception, while the furniture used to define the rooms are a dark oak. White room furniture with textile patches, custom-arranged in each room, dominate the central area. The generous impression of space provided by the loft is maintained, despite the visual and acoustic separation of the rooms from each other.

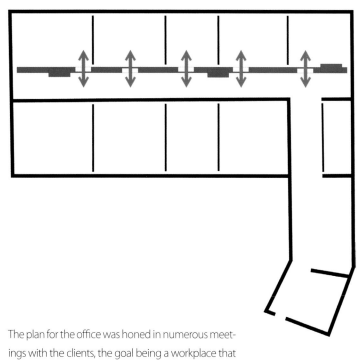

The plan for the office was honed in numerous meetings with the clients, the goal being a workplace that not only created a communicative climate, but also enabled concentrated and uninterrupted work.

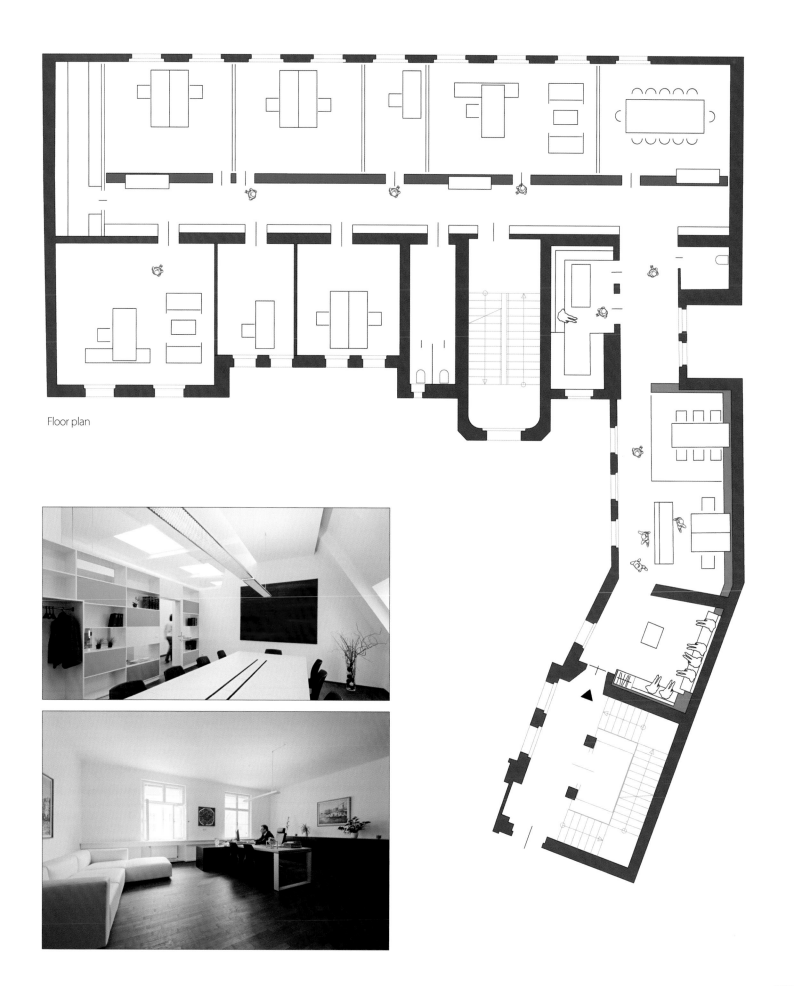

Floor plan

Cannon Design

The Power House, Renovation/Restoration

St. Louis, Missouri, USA   **Photographs:** Gayle Babcock Photography/Architectural Imageworks, LLC, unless otherwise indicated

After standing vacant for nearly 30 years, the St. Louis Municipal Power House building in downtown St. Louis opened as the new regional offices of Cannon Design in September 2008. All design, development, and construction management work for the restoration project was realized by the firm's own in-house teams. Constructed in 1928, the Power House was an original part of the Municipal Service Building complex that still occupies an entire block of downtown St. Louis – today providing parking space for city vehicles, a fire department and an electrical substation. The Power House component of the complex, designated as a landmark by the National Historic Register, provided coal-fired heating to a dozen downtown buildings before being decommissioned in 1980.

Although the building's exterior shell and original steel structure were fundamentally sound, reuse for a large architecture and engineering practice required a creative spatial solution that exploited the building's massive volume. Furthermore, the project represented an opportunity to rethink the implications of the physical office environment on the practice at a time of significant change in the profession at large and for the regional office specifically – the office was receiving projects of ever-increasing scale and working with new models of project delivery and new technologies and wanted a working environment that would support a more intuitive, flexible and open way of working.

Two new floor plates have been inserted inside the tall volume, thereby creating two extra floors and ample collaborative meeting space and workspaces for approximately 120 employees. The floor plates are separated from the external walls on two sides to preserve the full height of the arched windows on the north and east elevations, generating a partially full height gallery and exhibition space on the ground floor for use by the firm and the larger community. An elevator shaft, kitchenettes on each floor and two staircases have been inserted against the back wall in the northwest and southwest corners of the building. A model shop and materials library plus a boardroom have been excavated in the basement. On the roof, an oblong structure originally used to store coal conveyor equipment now houses another boardroom and staff lunchroom.

The original steel structure has been retained: a set of eight columns and trusswork while a new steel structure supports the second and third floors. These are faced in drywall and painted white. The interior of the original volume, essentially an empty shell, was completely restored and upgraded, with the installation of HVAC, plumbing, and electrical infrastructure. The building's "revival style" exterior, featuring tall, arched windows on three street façades and fine terra cotta detailing has been fully restored. External modifications include historically accurate replacement of windows in their original masonry openings and the creation of a 3,500 sqft garden.

Architecture:
Cannon Design

Floor area:
3,000 sqm (32,000 sqft)

Ground floor plan

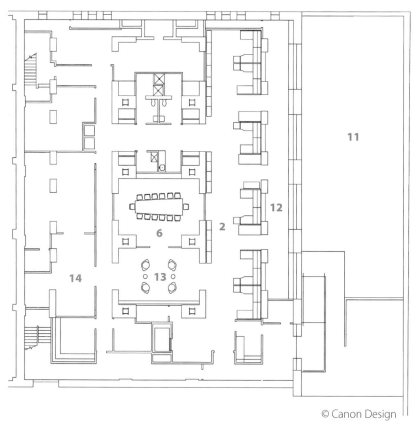

© Canon Design

+1 floor plan

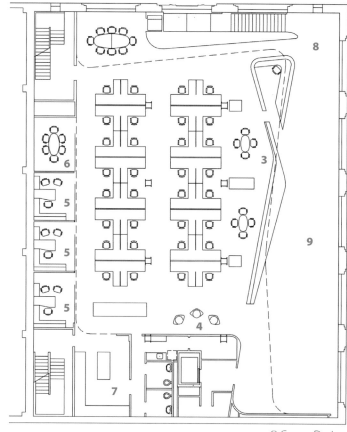

© Canon Design

KEY TO PLANS:

1. Reception
2. Gallery
3. Open office
4. Open team space
5. Crit space
6. Office
7. Conference
8. Work room
9. Open to Gallery below
10. Lunch room
11. Garden
12. Materials library
13. Design library
14. Model shop

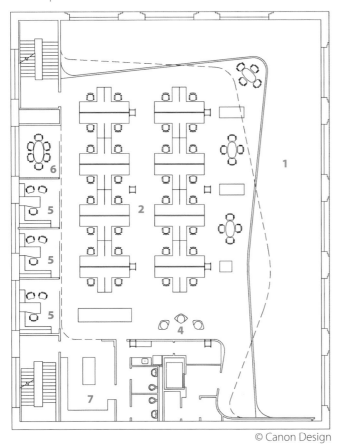

© Canon Design

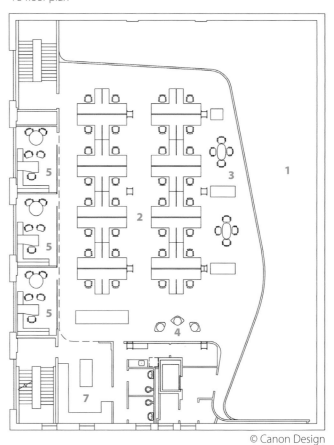

© Canon Design

© Patti Gabriel Photography

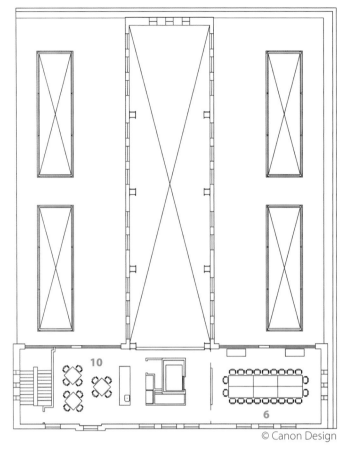

© Canon Design

PENTHOUSE/ROOF PLAN:

1. Reception
2. Gallery
3. Open office
4. Open team space
5. Crit space
6. Office
7. Conference
8. Work room
9. Open to gallery below
10. Lunch room
11. Garden
12. Materials library
13. Design library
14. Model shop

KlingStubbins

Autodesk AEC Headquarters

Waltham, Massachusetts, USA **Photographs:** Jeff Goldberg / Esto & KlingStubbins as credited

With the commission for the design of their new Waltham AEC Headquarters, Autodesk challenged the KlingStubbins architecture and construction team to not only create a new home for the Autodesk AEC division in an exciting and expressive space, but also to reinvent the design and construction process with an innovative Integrated Project Delivery agreement enabled with the latest Building Information Modeling tools.

The functional program included 55,000 sqft (5,110 sqm) of open workstations, private offices, collaborative spaces, and support spaces for the Autodesk staff, and a 5,000 sqft (464 sqm) Customer Briefing Center with a gallery and briefing rooms for Autodesk customers.

A LEED Platinum Certified project, sustainable design features include selecting a LEED Gold Certified base building, water and energy efficiency measures that reduce domestic water and energy consumption by over 30%, recycled non-toxic construction materials, C&D waste recycling, and interior planning that provides views to the outside and natural daylighting for all of the workspaces. The design solution expresses the Autodesk mission and values by exposing and featuring the building systems. A three-story floor opening visually connects the activities between all floors and provides a dramatic demonstration of the energy of the space to Autodesk visitors. Open workspaces and glass conference rooms provide visual connections and encourage collaboration. Open ceilings expose the building's structural and mechanical systems.

The project was delivered using an innovative BIM-Enabled Integrated Project Delivery (IPD) agreement. IPD is a progressive form of agreement – signed by the client, architect, and contractor – that safeguards shared common commitments to the success of the project including design quality, construction quality, schedule and budget. The IPD agreement enables and encourages unique project behaviors with a very high degree of proactive collaboration between the end users, designers, and builders. Both design innovation and process innovation were required in the conception and realization of this project. BIM technology offered the project team great tools to visualize, simulate, coordinate between teams and execute innovative design thinking. The Integrated Project Delivery (IPD) agreement enabled them to realize the full potential of the Building Information Modeling (BIM) tools. With an IPD agreement conventional process impediments, such as concerns for liability and fair compensation, are replaced with an empowered collaborative team culture motivated to use the best available tools to realize the full potential of the project. The final result was delivered on time and on budget, resulting from the creativity and hard work of the project team, magnified by the potential of BIM technology and enabled by IPD agreement.

Architecture and engineering design firm:
KlingStubbins

© Jeff Goldberg ▶

Autodesk

Autodesk technology helps people who change the world through design. Architecture, engineering, and construction projects around the world are transforming not just the landscape on which they sit, but the hearts and minds of those who see and use them. The Autodesk Gallery reveals the boundless artistry, sustainable design, and technological innovation behind some of today's most inspiring building projects.

Autodesk

Autodesk technology helps people who change the world through design. Architecture, engineering, and construction projects around the world are transforming not just the landscape on which they sit, but the hearts and minds of those who see and use them. The Autodesk Gallery reveals the boundless artistry, sustainable design, and technological innovation behind some of today's most inspiring building projects.

© Jeff Goldberg

The design solution expresses the Autodesk mission and values by exposing and featuring the building systems.

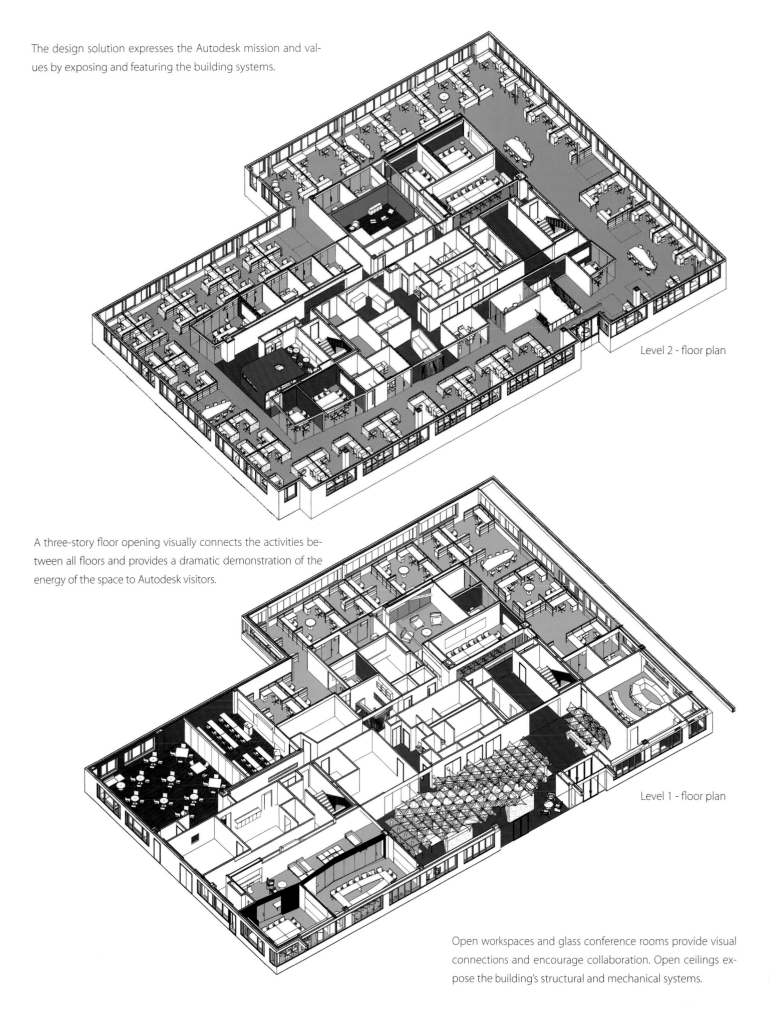

Level 2 - floor plan

A three-story floor opening visually connects the activities between all floors and provides a dramatic demonstration of the energy of the space to Autodesk visitors.

Level 1 - floor plan

Open workspaces and glass conference rooms provide visual connections and encourage collaboration. Open ceilings expose the building's structural and mechanical systems.

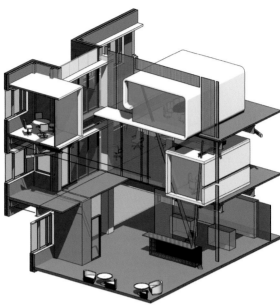

© Jeff Goldberg

© Jeff Goldberg

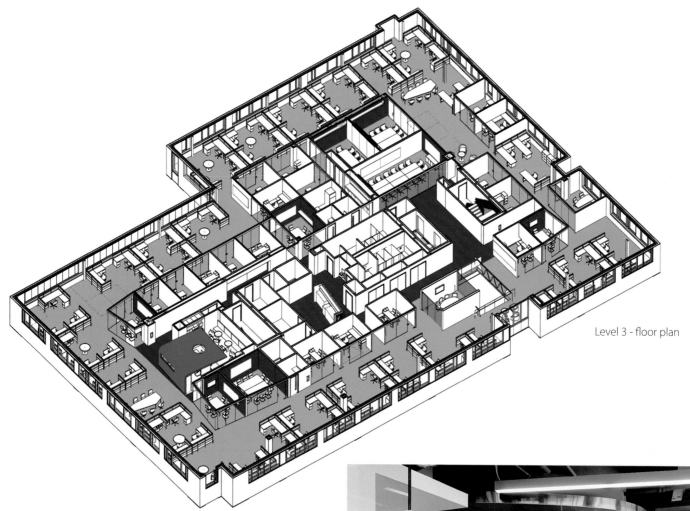

Level 3 - floor plan

© Jeff Goldberg

© Jeff Goldberg

© Jeff Goldberg

© Jeff Goldberg

Skylab Architecture

NORTH Office Interior

Portland, Oregon, USA

Photographs: Jeremy Bittermann

Architecture:
Skylab Architecture

NORTH is a branding agency that was seeking a new kind of office structure. To encourage collaborative thinking and fresh ideas, the space needed to respond to the way creative ideas are generated. The agency wanted a space that would stretch the parameters of their work.

Based on the idea of a polar research expedition to the frontier, a 10,000 square foot (929 sqm) "basecamp" was designed. The layout is based on social interactions that the designers saw as inspiring creative work – cooking, eating, lounging, and gaming. Workstations are replaced with modular structures, furniture and equipment defined around activity. Collaboration is based on portability and a cluster-on-demand structure in contrast to the traditional static office. The building, former home to a printing business, is on the National Register of Historic Places. The historic building shell is left untouched. Interior walls and structures come to the edge but are not fixed to the shell.

A single connection point provides fiber cable and utility functions. Pine panelling, raw steel and a carpet tile mural on the floor are the predominant interior features. Like an expedition that collects equipment to handle unknown challenges, the eclectic materiality of the movable office was selected for the ability to tackle different solutions to the design problem. A cantilevered think-tank module is elevated above the center of the space. It reveals a view of the West Hills through clerestory windows in the building. Similar to the NORTH creative process that reveals something about a client's brand that may have always been there but had not been communicated, this view had always been there, it was simply waiting for the viewpoint to be created.

Floral drapery and camouflage Fatboy beanbags allow for reflecting 'around a campfire'. A series of interspersed glass and metal panels define the editing module, two soundproof rooms without doors. Taking a universal icon for quick creative thought and communication, the media module is Post-it Note yellow. A commercial grade kitchen and adjacent dining area with picnic tables, wall mural, and topographic carpet tiles redefines out-of-doors inside. A visitor module of smoke walls and ice-white lighting is decorated with print, sound, and new media installations fostering an ever changing creative forum and connection with the local community.

Pine panelling, raw steel and a carpet tile mural on the floor are the predominant interior features. Like an expedition that collects equipment to handle unknown challenges, the eclectic materiality of the movable office was selected for the ability to tackle different solutions to the design problem.

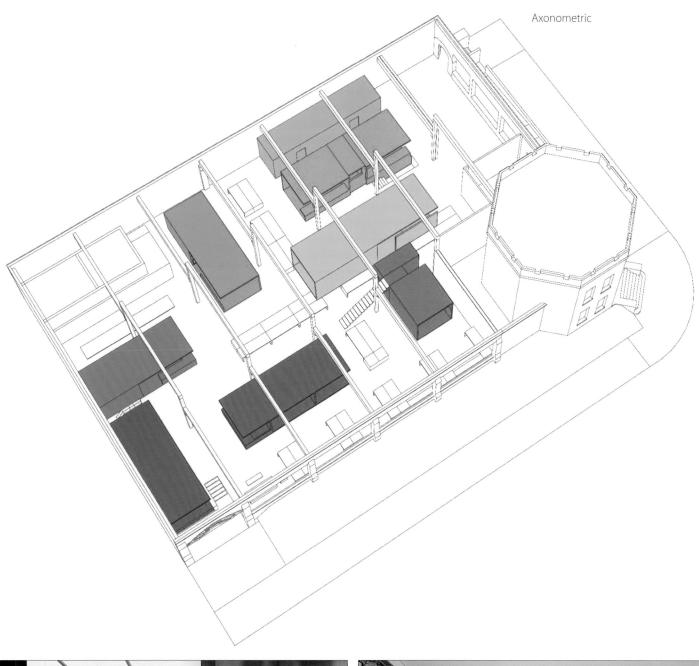

Axonometric

Neri & Hu Design and Research Office

The Black Box

Shanghai, China

Photographs: contributed by Neri&Hu Design and Research Office

The Black Box is a five-story office building located in the former French Concession in Shanghai, which also includes a street-level storefront space. On the ground level, two wooden façades make up the base of the building, one comprising the new Design Republic store and the other leading up to the Design Republic and Neri&Hu Design and Research office. The gallery and store on the ground level thus become an extension of the street. Above this glass and wooden exterior, a four-story dark façade is extruded and "cut" to reveal windows into the building.

The idea of the "Black Box" is the guiding concept behind the design, interpreted as a "black box" flight data recorder; it is used to represent the "storage" of conversation, ideas, thinking and research in the creative studio office. The black box also serves the function of protecting that recording in the event of a crash, fire or tragedy, analogous to the role of a design office servicing as a container of its intellectual production and protecting it from outside damage. The black box offers poignant, relevant and passionate design ideas with meaning and purpose to clients who may have had to face design tragedies in their lives. The ground floor in the form of a retail store displays some of these designed objects produced in the offices above, rendering it a window into the contents of the black box.

Within the Design Republic space the wooden box is pierced to reveal white boxes that frame the main display area. Private offices are contained within glass walls, just like within the original Design Republic office on the Bund. The upper two stories house the Neri&Hu Design and Research office space. The conference room consists of two stacked boxes, a wooden box on top of a white box.

Architecture:
Neri & Hu Design and Research Office

The Black Box is a five-story office building located in the former French Concession in Shanghai, which also includes a street-level storefront space. On the ground level, two wooden façades make up the base of the building, one comprising the new Design Republic store and the other leading up to the Design Republic and Neri&Hu Design and Research office.

The idea of the "Black Box" is the guiding concept behind the design, interpreted as a "black box" flight data recorder; it is used to represent the "storage" of conversation, ideas, thinking and research in the creative studio office.

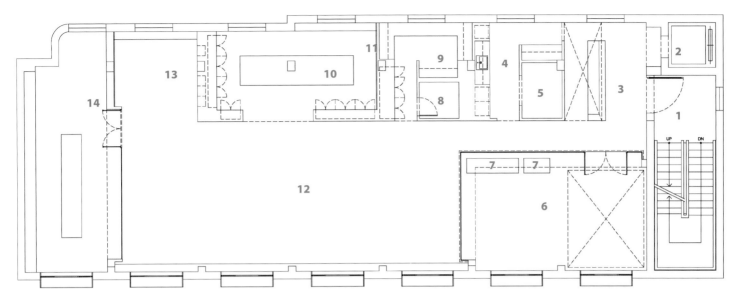

+4 FLOOR PLAN

1. Grand stair
2. Elevator
3. Floor reception
4. Kitchen
5. Server room
6. Main meeting room
7. Model display
8. Restroom
9. Print room
10. Graphics department
11. Pin-up wall
12. Open studios
13. Critique nook / nook library
14. Materials library

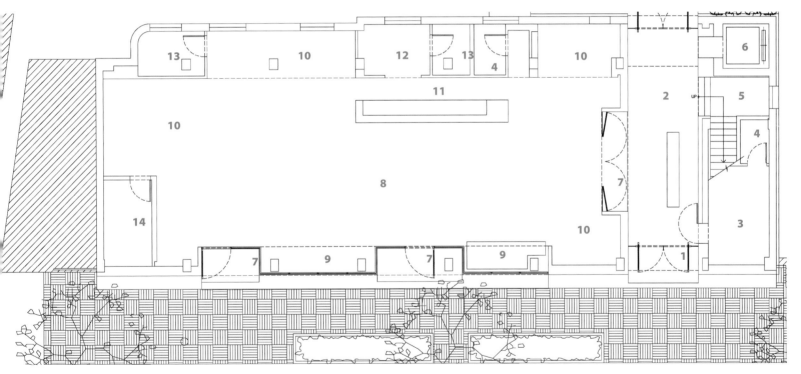

GROUND FLOOR PLAN

1. Building entrance
2. Main reception
3. Security
4. Restroom
5. Grand stair
6. Elevator
7. Retail entry
8. Showroom
9. Display
10. Shop-in-shop display
11. Cash wrap
12. Manager
13. Storage
14. Mechanical
15. Terrace
16. Garden

Randy Brown Architects

DATA

Omaha, Nebraska, USA

Photographs: Farshid Assassi

The brief for the interior design of these offices for a company that sells data online was for fresh new design that expressed the personality and outlook of the company.

The designers were immediately struck by the close personal relationships between all the employees. In order to encourage this culture they designed the working area as a large open plan space with workstations, a café and a gaming lounge. The second strategy of the design was to create a centrally located circulation element that would generate a distinctive atmosphere for the office and connect all the spaces. This was materialized as the porous central corridor formed by folded, fragmented green panels, which creates a diffuse space that leads from the entrance to the depth of the plan.

The design energy and most of the $28 per sqft budget was focused on three elements: the green corridor whose sculptural space is the central circulation element of the plan; a glass conference room wall with a design applied with a satin vinyl film that represents the endless data the company sells; galvanized metal shed wall panels which were used to express both the technological side of the business and the rural vernacular of the Midwest where this company was founded.

On a shoestring budget, the design creates a fresh new image for this leader of the information age and a dynamic people oriented working environment.

Architecture:
Randy Brown Architects

Design team:
Randy Brown, Andrea Kelly,
Brian Kelly, Neil Legband

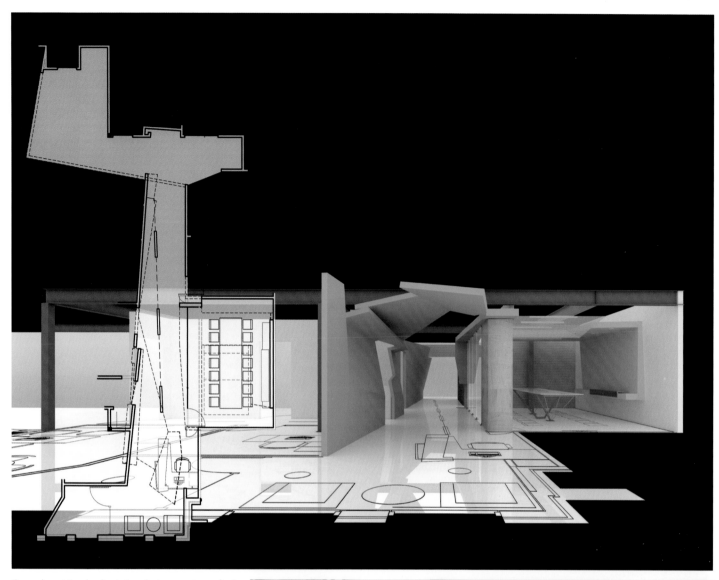

On a shoestring budget, the design creates a fresh new image for this leader of the information age and a dynamic people oriented working environment.

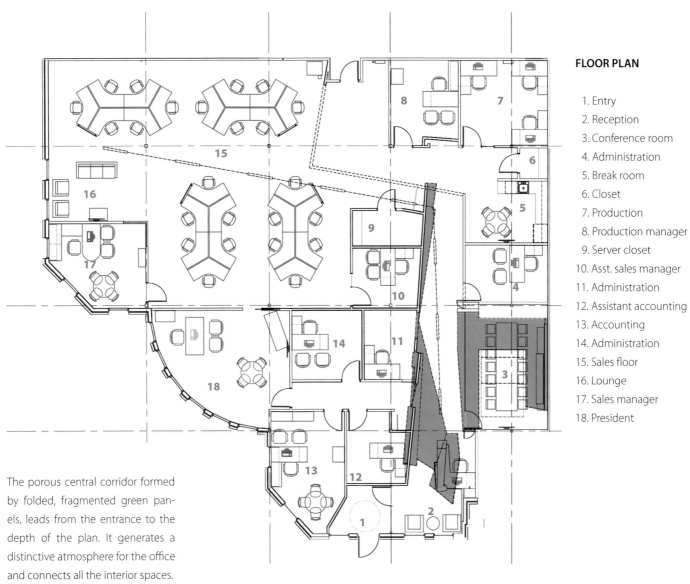

FLOOR PLAN

1. Entry
2. Reception
3. Conference room
4. Administration
5. Break room
6. Closet
7. Production
8. Production manager
9. Server closet
10. Asst. sales manager
11. Administration
12. Assistant accounting
13. Accounting
14. Administration
15. Sales floor
16. Lounge
17. Sales manager
18. President

The porous central corridor formed by folded, fragmented green panels, leads from the entrance to the depth of the plan. It generates a distinctive atmosphere for the office and connects all the interior spaces.

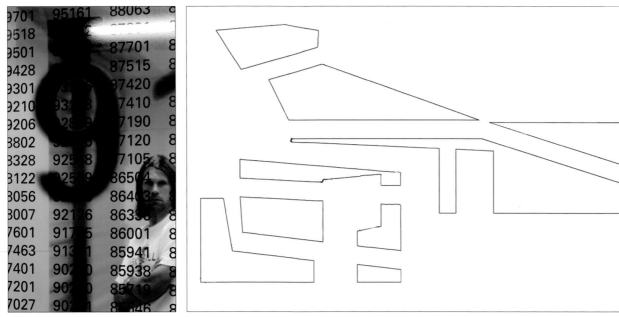

Unfolded

Origins Architects

Onesize Offices

Amsterdam, the Netherlands

Photographs: Stijn Stijl

Architecture:
Origins Architects

Construction:
KnE

In this low-budget conversion of an industrial building on the edge of Amsterdam into the workspaces and offices of the motion graphics design firm, Onesize, the firm's visual modeling work was the inspiration for the design.

The program included standard workspaces together with dark rooms for editing and projections. The existing building, a top-lit industrial hangar, was an open and airy space which the architects saw would lend itself to the insertion of a central volume around which the work of the company could be carried out. Whereas projection rooms and editing suites are often segregated from other activities and located in basements or residual spaces, in this project they have been placed in the very center of the plan, representing their position and importance in the firm's activities, aligned along the central axis of the space within a striking secondary structure. This structure, inspired by the visual modeling activities of the firm, is a series of polygonal sculptural forms realized in low-grade timber multiplex board which transforms the program into an interesting shape while subdividing the space to create a clear layout. The design of these objects began with complex forms which were progressively simplified through the design process. As Jamie van Lede, the founder of Origins Architects, commented: 'We started out with more complex shapes, but the simpler they became, the better the result'. Origins Architects specialize in sustainable building, so they were also keeping an eye on the environmental impact of the project. By doing so, they developed sculptural volumes whose construction could be realized with nominal wastage of the raw materials.

The three central structures house, respectively, the meeting space, projection room and editing suite, with degrees of permeability of their outer shells which vary in relation to the activity housed within. Thus the editing suite and projection room volumes are opaque on three sides with glazed end walls permitting visual connection to surrounding spaces, while the meeting space is defined by series of porticoes which suggest, rather than enclose, its volume.

Key decisions on the materialization of the interior spaces were taken in consideration of the acoustic, lighting and fireproofing requirements. Low grade spruce multiplex boarding – usually used under carpeting – was used for the central structure. Besides the cost issue, the architects strongly believed that the juxtaposition of high definition detailing and a low grade material would make both stand out better. This contrast is also echoed in the formal relationship between the existing building and the new sculptural objects. Wood and concrete, fine detailing against coarse materials, dark and light are the juxtapositions that define the aesthetics of this project.

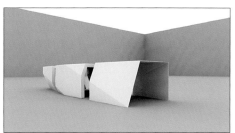

The program for this conversion of an industrial building on the edge of Amsterdam into the workspaces and offices of the motion graphics design firm, Onesize, included standard workspaces together with dark rooms for editing and projections.

Floor plan

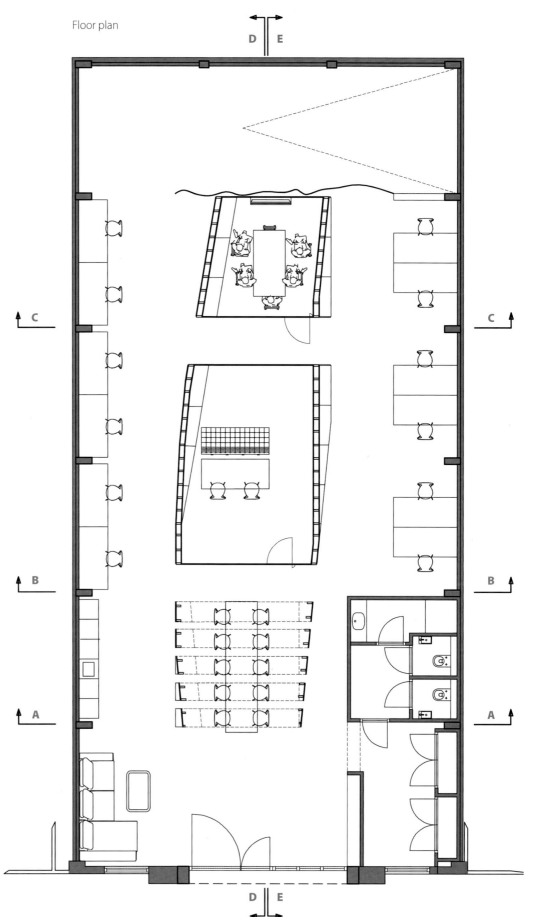

1. Projector
2. Classic mac
3. Classic camera
4. 8mm editor
5. Paintgun
6. Toy robot
7. Film rolls
8. Cameras
9. 3x joysticks
10. Atari console

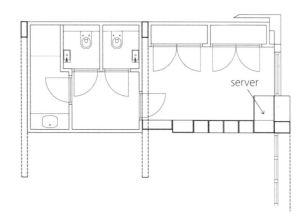

server

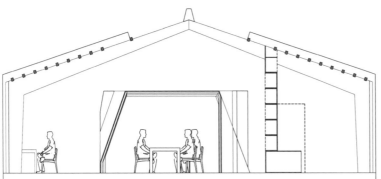

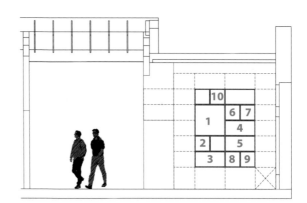

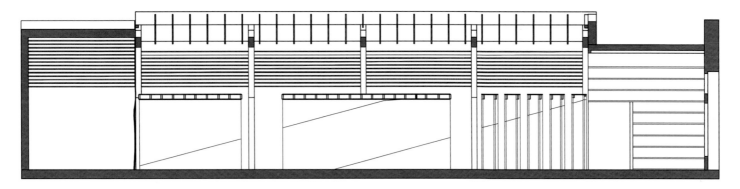

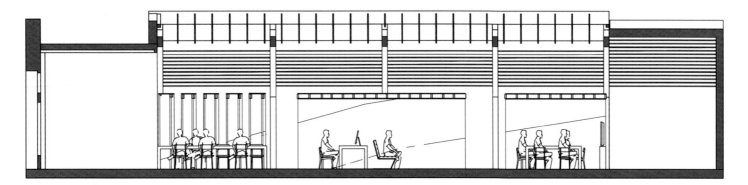

Albert France-Lanord Architects

Pionen – White Mountain

Stockholm, Sweden

Photographs: Åke E:son Lindman

Albert France-Lanord Architects were commissioned to convert a 1,200 square meter decommissioned atomic bunker, located in the granite substrate 30 meters under the Vita Berg Park in Stockholm, to house server halls and offices for the internet service provider Bahnhof AB.

The starting point of the project was to consider the rock as a living organism. Humans attempt to acclimatize themselves to this foreign world by bringing the best elements from the surface: light, plants, water and technology. The architects, for their part, were excited to work with spaces that weren't inherently orthogonal, their geometry being determined by the internal geometry of the rock. The main office volume is not a traditional space limited by planar surfaces but rather it is defined as a void within a mass.

The interior design was inspired by the aesthetics of science fiction films, mostly 'Silent Running' and James Bond films with Ken Adams sets. Strong contrasts were generated between rooms where the rock dominates over the human being and rooms where the human being has taken over completely. The lighting design was a critical and particularly challenging facet of the project. In order to help employees orient themselves in time and space within this fully enclosed environment, the lighting has been designed to be as varied as possible.

One can describe the project process in five different phases: planning; demolition of the existing interiors and controlled explosions to create extra space; structural reinforcement of the cave; technical service installations; internal fit-out; finishes and furnishing.

The client had a strong vision from the outset and the impressive outcome of the project was only possible because of their persistence, uncompromising attitude and the fluent communication and understanding between all parties involved in the project.

Architecture:
Albert France-Lanord Architects

Design assistants:
Frida Öster and Jonatan Blomgren

Client:
Bahnhof AB

Floor area:
1200 sqm (12,900 sqft)

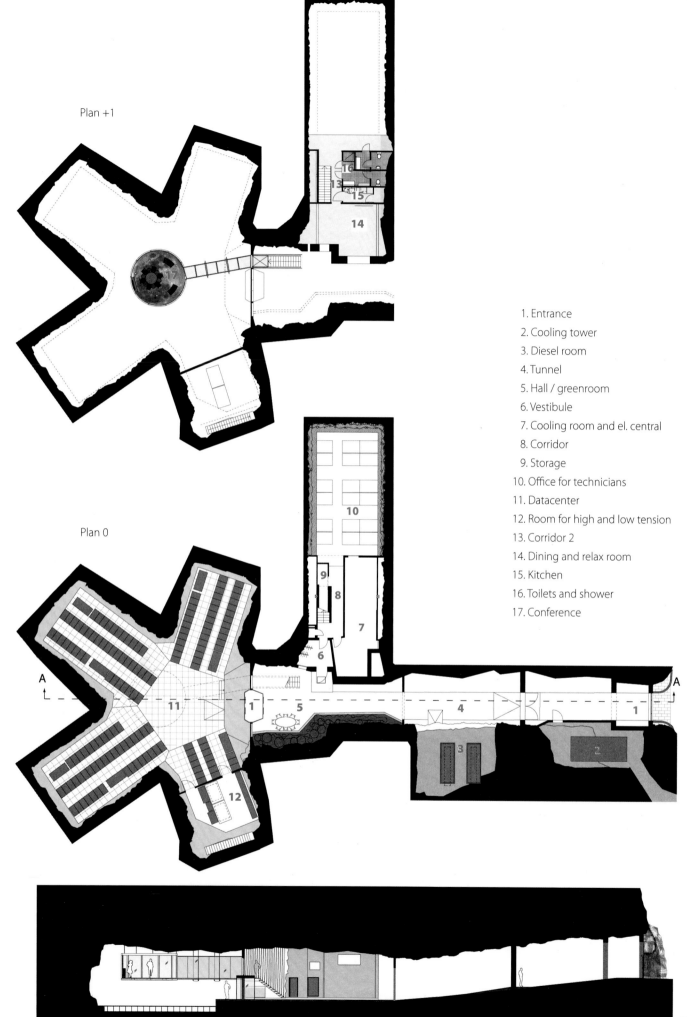

Plan +1

Plan 0

1. Entrance
2. Cooling tower
3. Diesel room
4. Tunnel
5. Hall / greenroom
6. Vestibule
7. Cooling room and el. central
8. Corridor
9. Storage
10. Office for technicians
11. Datacenter
12. Room for high and low tension
13. Corridor 2
14. Dining and relax room
15. Kitchen
16. Toilets and shower
17. Conference

Section A-A

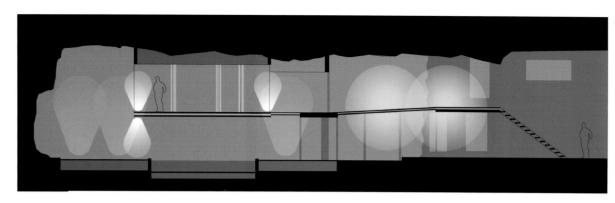

Longitudinal section 1

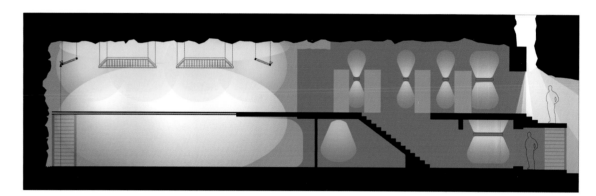

Longitudinal section 2

The interior design was inspired by the aesthetics of science fiction films, mostly 'Silent Running' and James Bond films with Ken Adams sets. Strong contrasts were generated between rooms where the rock dominates over the human being and rooms where the human being has taken over completely.

Crea International

CheBanca! Branch Offices

various locations throughout Italy

Photographs: Crea International

Crea International has designed the new and surprising retail format for the Mediobanca group, Che-Banca!, a multichannel distribution model based on internet banking, customer service and new generation "light" branches.

The design of the new branches emphasizes the consultancy, DIY transaction and self-education activities, placing the consumer at the center of the process.

The "Natural Tech" concept designed by Crea International is inspired by "the rules of simplicity" by John Maeda. This influential design idea propounds that the objects that surround us should be simplified to the maximum possible degree. The atmosphere of CheBanca! recalls the warmth and light of sunshine while the layout recalls the logical organization of the solar system with the client at the center. The "Natural Tech" of CheBanca! is intended to convey an ethical and transparent financial institution, an apparently technology free environment where direct human contact is at the forefront.

The yellow color that permeates the environment recalls sunshine and the aniline treated wood suggests a straightforward approach, while the metacrylic panels printed with a honeycomb texture create a friendly atmosphere.

According to Massimo Fabbro, managing partner of Crea International, "With the design of CheBanca! we materialized the oxymoron "innovation and reassurance" through a formal alchemy that is new to the banking context. An alchemy made up of space organization and a completely unique furniture shape together with reassuring and warm codes."

The innovations in this project are various: first of all, the layout with a central base point and perimeter connection booths. An open and fluid space is generated at the center of which is a counter from where the store staff move to attend the customers. At the entrance, the consumer is directed to the multitasking connection booths where any banking operation can be performed either in DIY mode or with the support of store staff, upon request. Interactive walls display product offers and information about local cultural events. There are two areas for relaxing: a coffee bar and a children's garden. CheBanca! represents a banking concept with great communicative power in which the designers have used formal and layout innovations to boost the attraction potential. The CheBanca! design concept transforms the retail banking branch from a place for realizing transactions into a social space.

Physical brand design:
Crea International

Design team:
client leader: massimo fabbro
strategy director: viviana rigolli
design director: marco michele rossi
project director: sara rimini
designer: andrea borsetto
architect: marcela mangupli
graphic designers: ester gregori
serena di fidio

According to Massimo Fabbro, managing partner of Crea International, "With the design of Che-Banca! we materialized the oxymoron "innovation and reassurance" through a formal alchemy that is new to the banking context.

An alchemy made up of space organization and a completely unique furniture shape together with reassuring and warm codes.

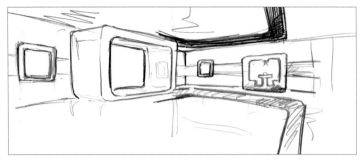
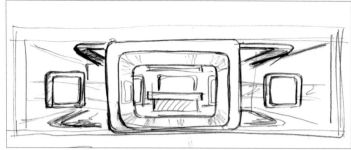
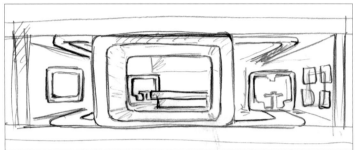

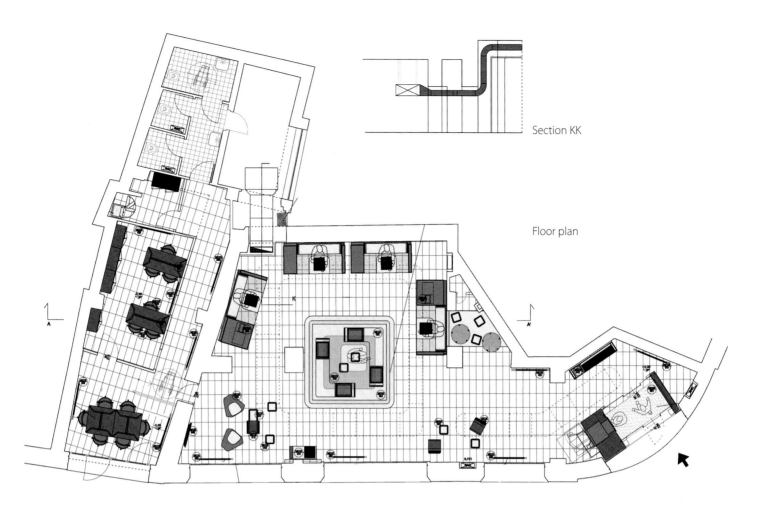

Section KK

Floor plan

Ippolito Fleitz Group

Agency Bruce B./Emmy B.

Stuttgart, Germany

Photographs: Zooey Braun

Bruce B./Emmy B. is a prestigious design agency specializing in communication design and events. When Ippolito Fleitz moved into new premises on the Augustenstraße in Stuttgart, Bruce B./Emmy B. – long-term collaborators of the architects – decided to join them in the same building, and commissioned them to design the interior for their agency.

The five-story building at Augustenstraße 87 dates from the Wilhelminian period and was originally built to house an industrial laundry. Bruce B. /Emmy B. moved into an almost 500 sqm (5,380 sqft) space on the third floor.

The architects' aim in designing the interior for this agency was to translate into architecture the essence of its work. Objects and design elements initially appear to be in diametric opposition, yet strike a harmonious balance throughout. They are emblematic of Bruce B./Emmy B.'s approach of responding to their clients with an open, strategic mindset and an excellent command of antithetical thinking. Antitheses attract the visitor's attention from the very first moment of entering the agency, beginning with the shape of the reception desk. It is crafted in exposed concrete, which displays its materiality in the visible texture of the timber plank shuttering. The concrete form is topped by a white, lacquered surface. Antithetical details are also present in the adjoining conference rooms – usually the second point of call for the agency's clients. The walls of the smaller conference room are panelled with maritime pine boards. Narrow yellow grooves refine their appearance, which would normally invoke simple packing crates, transforming them into attractive wall panelling. The large conference room next door is dominated by a long conference table with randomly spaced table legs breaking up the sober impression it would otherwise have made. Directing your gaze towards the ceiling of the reception area and conference rooms allows you to take in another unusual detail: Stucco elements have been added to the ceiling joists, recalling the cosiness of an old apartment building in the very midst of this industrial landscape.

The atelier itself is an open-plan room of 250 sqm (2,690 sqft). The space is characterized by the original ceiling joists, which were restored and connected with the ceiling by means of a cavetto. Indirect lighting in the interstitial spaces creates a diffused light that is ideal for work. Shelving units hanging from the ceiling are aligned with the ceiling joists, delimiting the workstations. The workstations themselves are solid oak tables, most of which the client already had at his disposal. The furnishings create individual units with plenty of free space in between. The units are placed together in groups of two or three to form islands within the space. The resultant effect is a mix of open-plan office and semi-enclosed cubicles. This layout is emphasised by the circles of carpet that reinforce the island groupings.

Architecture:
Ippolito Fleitz Group

Client:
Bruce B./Emmy B.

The architects' objective in designing the interior was to translate into architecture the essence of the agency's work.

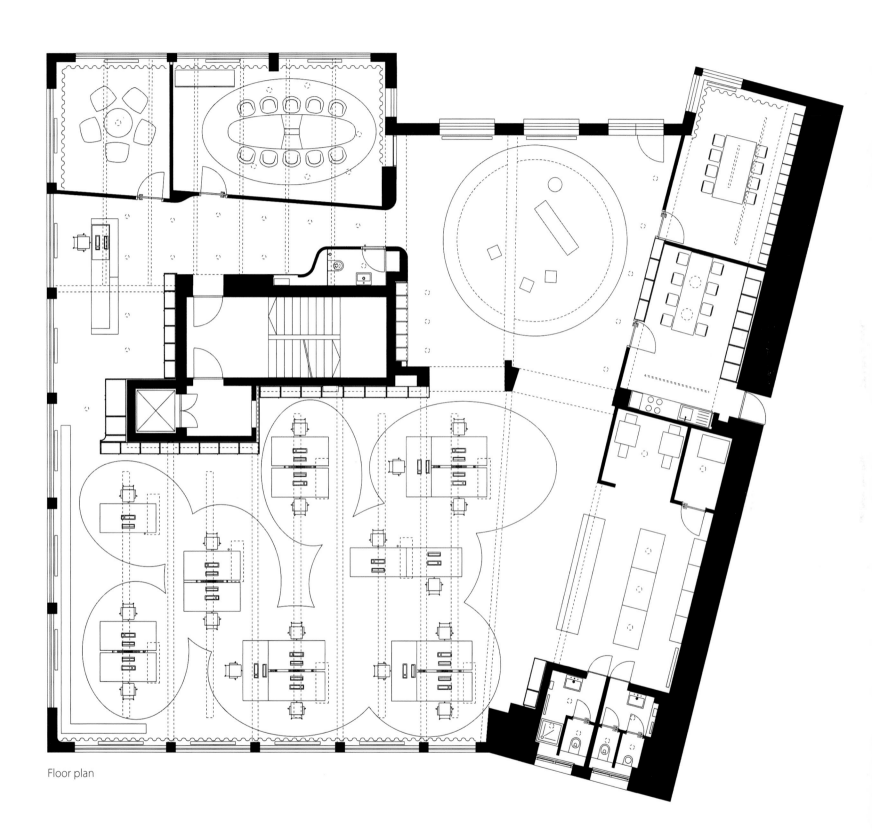

Floor plan

Shelving units hanging from the ceiling are aligned with the ceiling joists, delimiting the workstations.

The resultant effect is a mix of open-plan office and semi-enclosed cubicles. This layout is emphasised by the circles of carpet that reinforce the island groupings.

Johnson Chou Inc.

Red Bull Canadian Headquarters

Toronto, Canada

Photographs: contributed by Johnson Chou Inc.

The Red Bull slogan, "Red Bull gives you Wings", was taken as the starting point for this conversion project which consisted of transforming an existing building in Toronto into the Red Bull Music Academy – a music academy financed and run by the drinks brand – with a posterior conversion of the same space into the company's Canadian headquarters. The notion of "wings", suggesting movement, freedom and revitalization, combined with Red Bull's corporate philosophy evolved into a metaphor of transformation – of personal and architectural transformation.

Both phases were designed simultaneously together with the planning of the second phase construction works. The architects decided to modify the original building fabric as little as possible for cost reasons in order to focus on improving the existing services and implementing new architectural elements. The Music Academy encapsulates Red Bull's corporate philosophy of mentorship instead of sponsorship. The new space, both as the Academy and later as the Canadian Headquarters of the brand is intended to function as a forum for the exchange of ideas, an inspirational hub where knowledge and experience is gained and disseminated and the participants transformed through the experience. The design concept used for the Music Academy and Headquarters was a metaphorical representation of the spaces as vessels for transformation: both as significant events in the lives of the participants and experientially, with engaging, interactive architectural elements. The notion of "vessels" and "transformation" is represented at many levels, from the smallest detail to the overall space. Forms and details evocative of the brand's ideals are gradually revealed as one moves through the space. The metaphor of the "vessel for transformation" appears in various forms, in the memento boxes on the atrium wall, the entrance corridor, the glass enclosed wooden reception desk, pivoting gallery walls, and the various meeting rooms.

The architectural elements of the space are "vessels" created to support the activities within, designed to stimulate creativity. Gathering spaces from enclosed, private rooms to open casual areas for impromptu meetings provide opportunities for the exchange of ideas.

The wing-like curved glass partition walls of the private offices animate the space, creating pattern and repetition. A new double-height atrium space with a custom-designed perforated steel spiral stair was created to link the two floors. Second floor meeting rooms contain bar-like, sunken, and formal meeting areas.

Architecture:
Johnson Chou Inc.

Lead designer:
Johnson Chou

Project designer/manager:
Silke Stadtmueller

Designers:
Can V. Bui, Heather Shute

Structural engineers:
Blackwell Bowick

KEY TO PLANS:

1. Entrance stair
2. Transition tube
3. Waiting / Library
4. Reception
5. Gallery
6. Atrium
7. Dining / Lunch area
8. Kitchen
9. Private offices
10. Open workstation
11. Team office
12. Printing storage
13. Bar meeting area
14. Lounge meeting area
15. Boardroom
16. Exterior deck

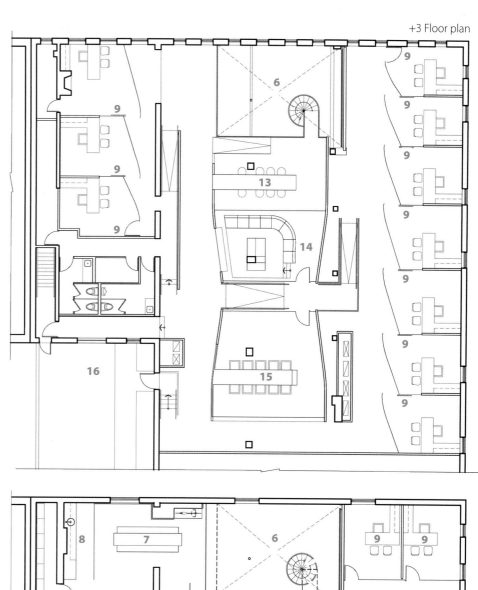

+3 Floor plan

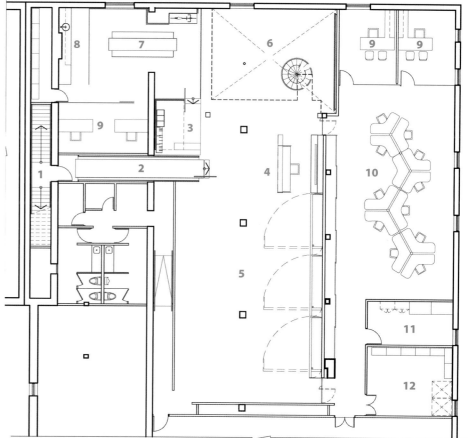

+2 Floor plan (access)

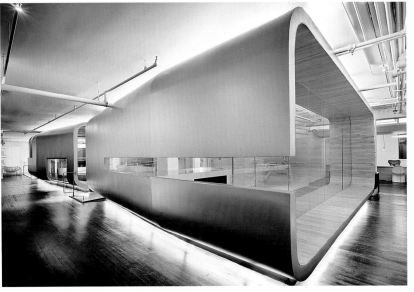